Australian Paintings

Artworks

by

Marji Hill

Published by The Prison Tree Press 2024

Cover: "Tulip Farm" by Marji Hill
ISBN 978-0-9756571-0-2 (paperback)
ISBN 978-0-9756571-1-9 (eBook)

The Prison Tree Press
Suite 124
1-10 Albert Avenue
Broadbeach, Queensland 4218

https://marjihill.com
https://www.fastselfpublishing.com

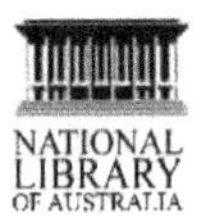

A catalogue record for this work is available from the National Library of Australia

Disclaimer
All the material contained in this book is provided for educational and informational purposes only. No responsibility can be taken for any results or outcomes resulting from the use of this material.

While every care has been taken to trace and acknowledge copyright the publishers tender their apologies for any accidental infringement where copyright has proved untraceable.

Every attempt has been made to provide information that is both accurate and effective, however, the author does not assume any responsibility for the accuracy or use/misuse of this information.

Table of Contents

Preface

I acknowledge the Traditional Custodians of Country throughout Australia and their connections to land, sea, and community. I pay my respect to elders, past, present, and emerging and extend my respect to all First Nations peoples today.

In the spirit of reconciliation, my mission is to increase understanding between the First Nations and other Australians and to provide people from all over the globe some basic understanding of Australia's first people, their history, and cultures.

Not only have I done this through my books but much of my artwork also has to do with Australia's First Nations people.

Painting has always been part and parcel of my life, so I invite you to step into my world of art. I'm thrilled to unveil this collection of paintings which range from pieces I made in my teenage years to creations of today. Journey alongside me as I showcase a diverse array of my paintings.

My canvases serve as a mirror reflecting the rich tapestry of Australian society, delving into themes such as black/white relations, reconciliation, our nation's hidden past, and the allure of gold discovery.

Yet amidst the serious issues confronting Australian society I sprinkle moments of fun and light-heartedness. I love to capture the essence of land and sea and I revel in exploring the kaleidoscope of colours that nature generously bestows upon us.

The seed for this book was planted when I made an art calendar. I hastily assembled some of my paintings without any thought to documentation.

It dawned on me then that my artworks needed a platform where the stories behind each creation could unfold. Thus, this book was born, a labour of love aimed at providing not only a comprehensive review of a lot of my life's work but also a treasure trove of inspiration for my cherished followers.

So here it is. Dive in, and let the journey begin! Enjoy!

And finally, thank you Eddie Dowd, for helping me get this book into its final form and ready for publication.

Marji Hill

Chapter 1

Political

"Eureka Stockade"

Collection: Art Gallery of Ballarat
Medium: Oil on canvas

"Eureka Stockade", a large (213 x 167cm) oil painting was part of the 2004-2005 Art Gallery of Ballarat's Travelling Exhibition *Eureka Revisited: The Contest of Memories*. This exhibition travelled to Melbourne, Canberra and Ballarat and was part of the 150-year celebration of the Eureka Stockade.

In December 1854 gold miners at Ballarat in Victoria initiated an armed uprising and battled to defend their rights against the colonial government and authorities. Their underlying principles were equality, fair treatment by the government, and the right to take part in the government process.

The inspiration for this painting evolved when I started the research for the book *Six Australian Battlefields* which I co-authored with Al Grassby.

The book was published in 1988 by Angus and Robertson and then a decade later it was re-published by Allen & Unwin as a paperback. One of the battles featured in the book was the Eureka Stockade.

When I started work on the book, I was also doing formal art training at the then Canberra School of Art (which in 1992 became ANU School of Art & Design).

While doing my Post Graduate Diploma in Painting I was given an art studio and this is where I created the painting "Eureka Stockade".

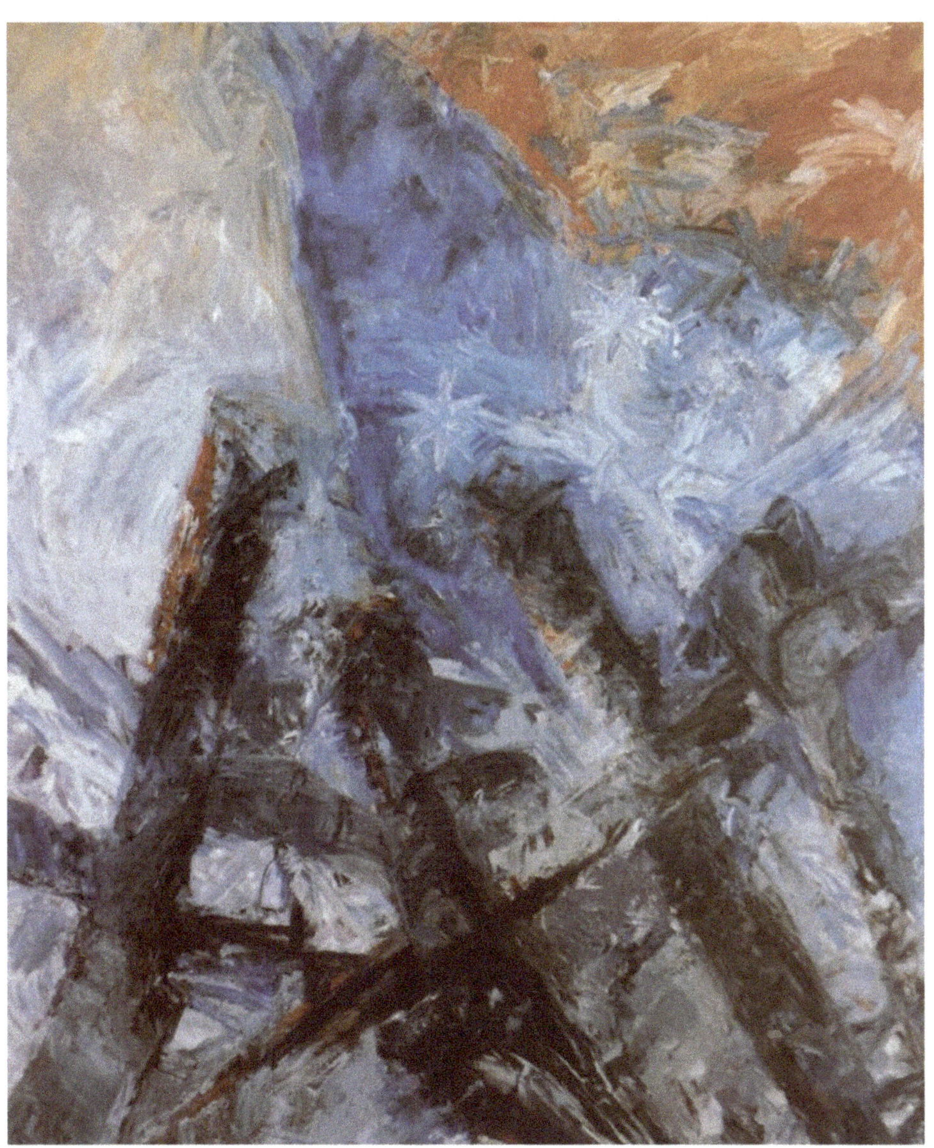

"The Southern Cross Flag"

Collection: Art Gallery of Ballarat
Medium: Oil/collage

At 11am on 29 November 1854 in the lead-up to the Eureka Stockade, the Southern Cross flag was raised which is still today seen as the symbol of Eureka, democracy and defiance.

The inspiration for "The Southern Cross Flag", a large painting 213 x 167cm, was another outcome of working on the book *Six Australian Battlefields*.

When Ballarat was celebrating its 150-year anniversary of the Eureka Stockade friends of mine visiting Ballarat told me they saw the painting hanging in the Ballarat Town Hall.

I produced a lot of Eureka paintings. A collection of these paintings today is held at the Ballarat campus of the Australian Catholic University.

Other paintings on the Eureka theme are in my book *Shadows of Gold: Eureka and the Birth of Australian Democracy*.

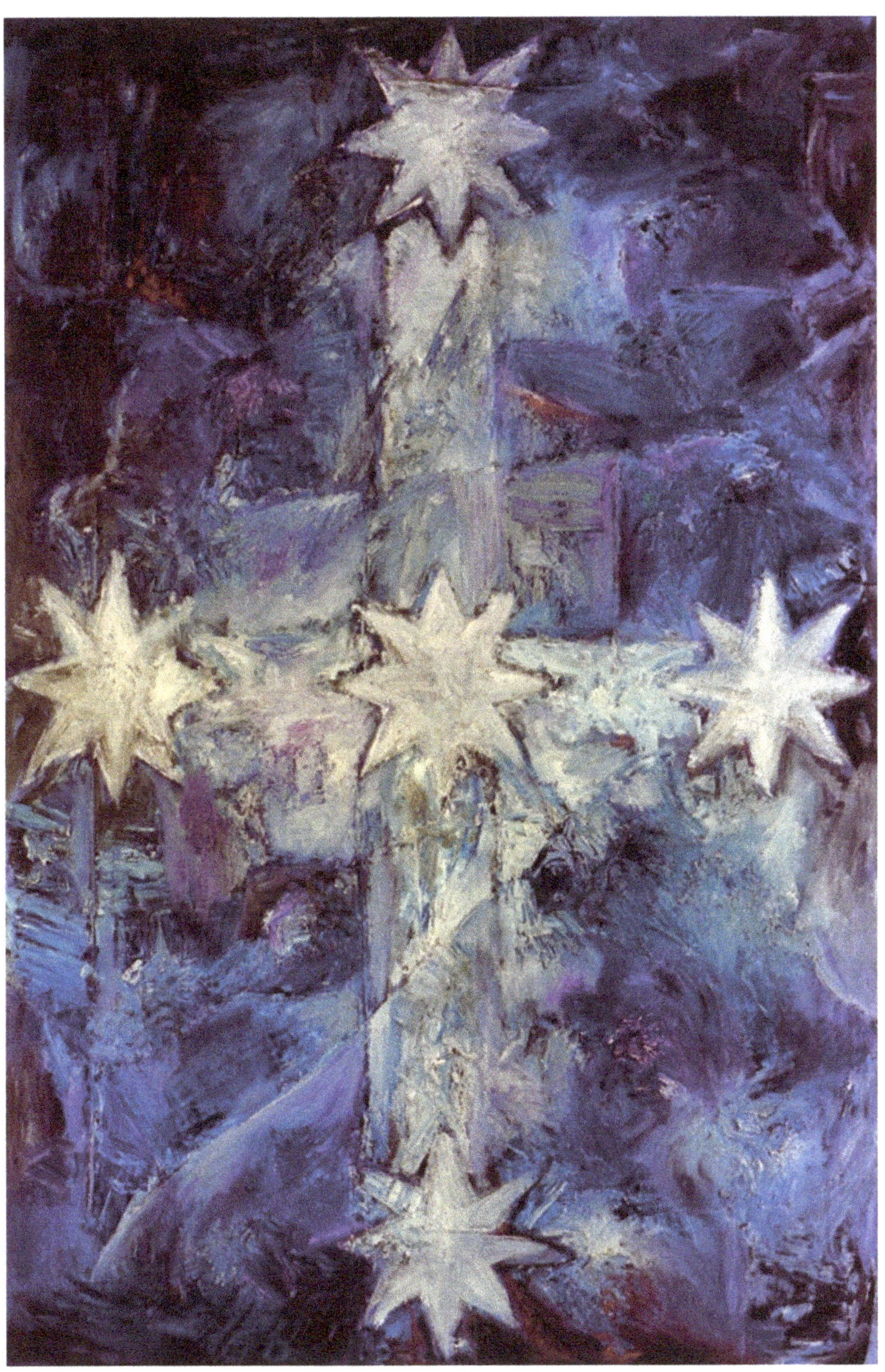

"British Soldier"

Medium: Gouache on paper

From 1788 when the British occupied the great southern continent, British regiments had a strong presence.

As British settlement became more established, British landholders had an insatiable greed for more land and there was unplanned and unregulated occupation of thousands of hectares of land beyond the Blue Mountains. Bathurst, for instance, became a military and supply base. Tensions with the Wiradjuri people developed as the red-coated soldiers arrived with convicts. At gun point the newcomers took over the best land and the permanent water supplies.

Violent conflict on the Australian frontier had started and from this time on, Australia experienced constant warfare on its frontier.

It became clear that the British, with the help of the British soldiers, were taking over the continent and were going to occupy the lands belonging to Australia's First Nations people.

And in the lead-up to the Eureka Stockade, seeds of rebellion were everywhere. At the end of November 1854, troops from the 12th Regiment arrived in Melbourne. When this news reached Ballarat the first digger militia was quickly formed to intercept them. The British troops, commanded by Captain H. C. Wise, brought cannon and in the early hours of Sunday morning 3 December 1854, British forces were assembled for a surprise attack on the Stockade.

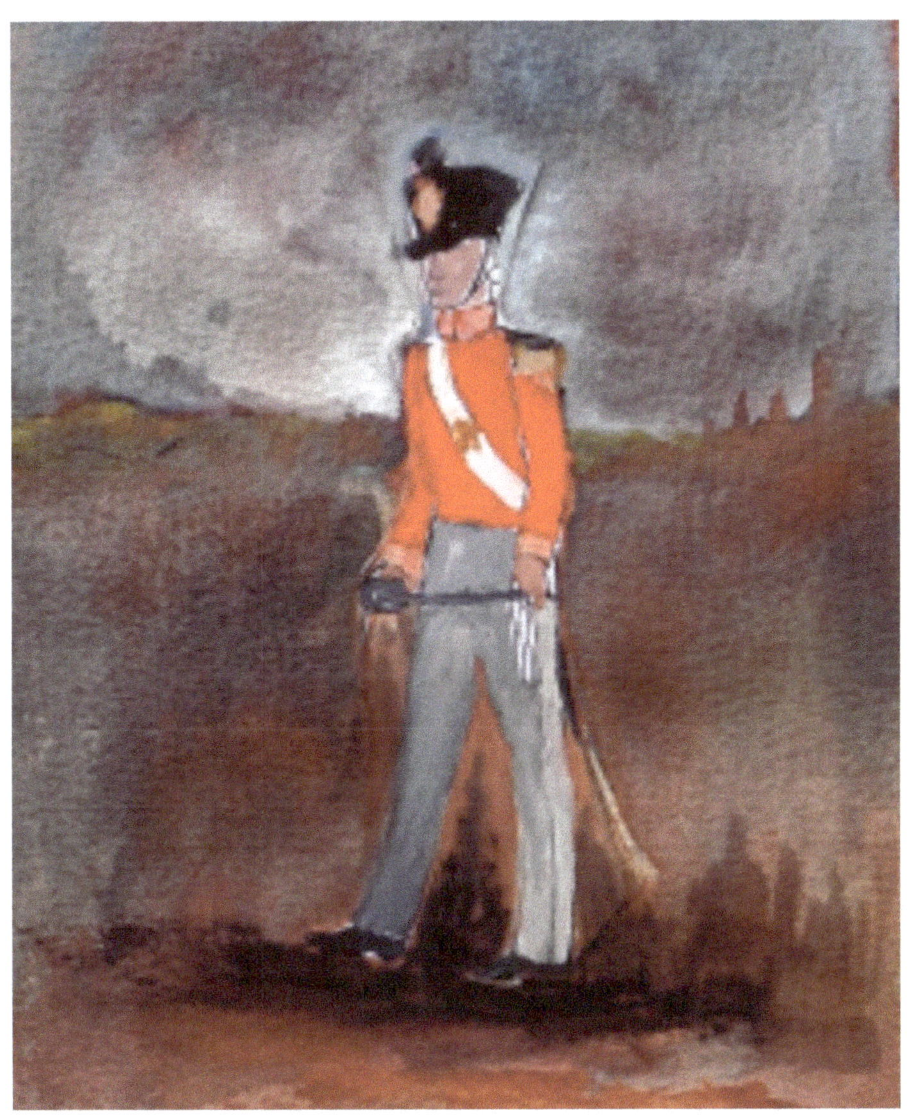

Chapter 2

Gold

"Jupiter's Lucky Strike"

Collection: Citigold Corporation
Medium: Oil

"Jupiter's Lucky Strike" celebrates the discovery of gold by First Nations boy, Jupiter Mosman in 1871 at Charters Towers in North Queensland.

Commissioned by the Citigold Corporation, the painting today resides in their offices at Charters Towers. It hung for many years in the foyer of Jupiter's Casino in Townsville until the casino was eventually sold, becoming The Ville Resort-Casino.

It is a large painting 152.4 x 182.88 cm.

On 23 December 1871 at what became Charters Towers, a storm was threatening. Three gold prospectors Hugh Mosman, George Clarke and James Fraser and their First Nations horse boy, Jupiter, were preparing to set up camp close to the high, rocky, tower-like formation.

Before they could unload their packhorse, a terrific clap of thunder frightened the horse and it galloped away into the bush. When daylight came the prospectors were anxious to find the spooked animal and the equipment it carried away.

The care of the horses was Jupiter's job and his responsibility to retrieve them. When he found the horse, he tethered it and knelt by the stream of water to get a drink. As he did so he saw the early morning sunlight glistening on a small stone in the water. It was gold and it was Christmas Eve 1871.

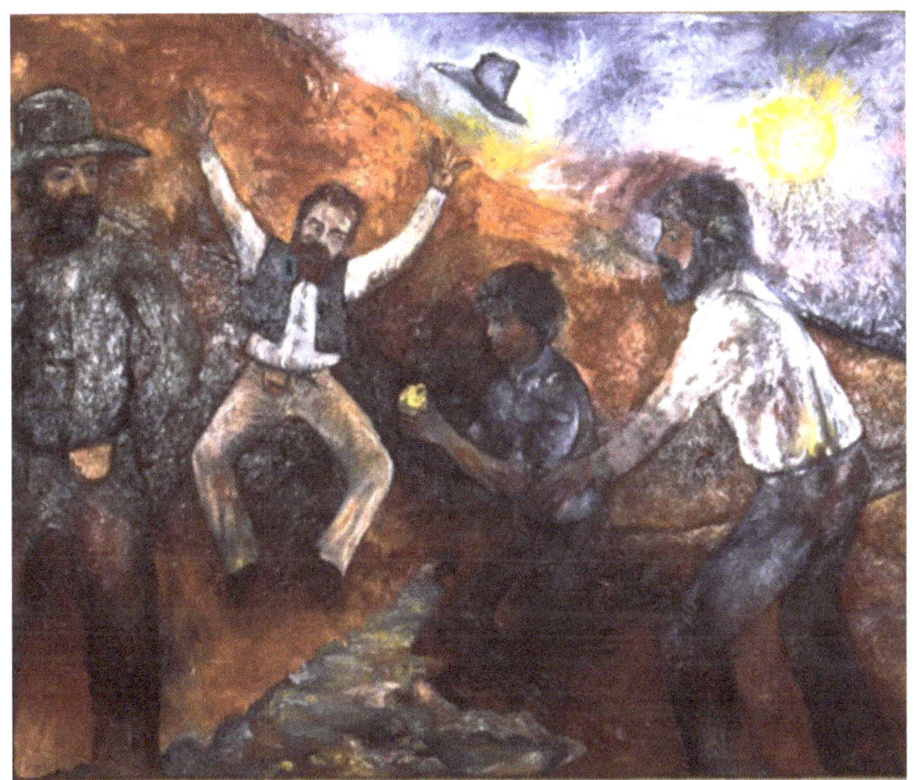

"Jupiter Mosman"

Collection: World Theatre, Charters Towers
Medium: Oil on canvas

In 1997 my partner, Alex Barlow, and I made a memorable trip to Charters Towers in North Queensland.

During our time there, we came across a small, archival photograph of Jupiter Mosman in The Northern Miner Charters Towers. This find stirred our interest in the Jupiter story.

Alex began his research into Jupiter Mosman. I created a portrait which was based on the small archival photograph.

The Citigold Corporation commissioned the painting, and it now hangs in the World Theatre at Charters Towers in North Queensland.

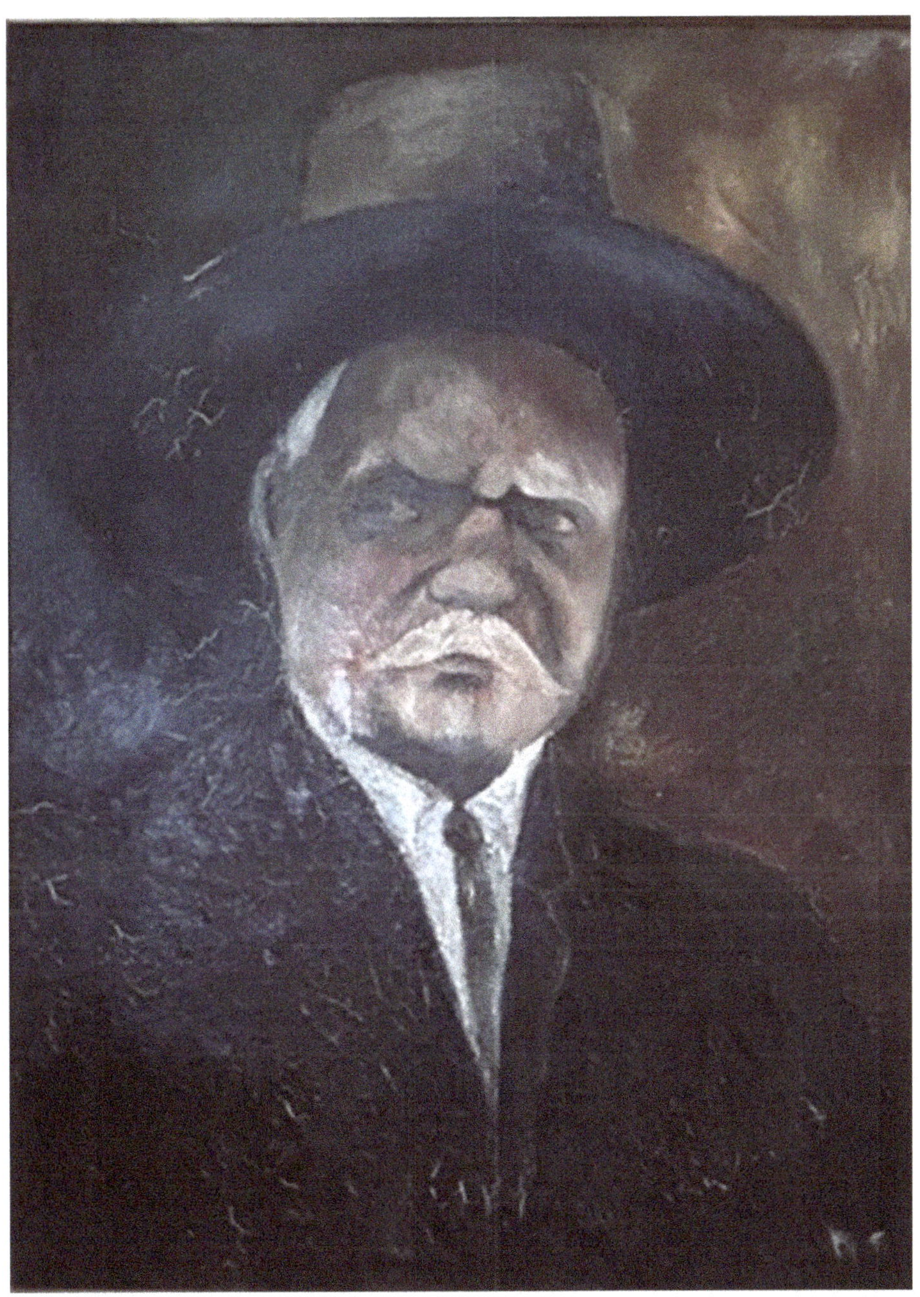

"Down the Decline"

Collection: Citigold Corporation
Medium: Oil on canvas

On one of our trips to Charters Towers in North Queensland, we visited the Citigold Corporation's mine site. We went down the main 1,400-metre-long access tunnel which is 200 metres deep.

While deep down in the decline I took photographs. These images of gold in the rock became the inspiration for my painting *"Down the Decline."* (approx.106 x 137 cm).

The goldfield is centred on and surrounds the town of Charters Towers.

The Citigold Corporation's gold deposit at Charters Towers is Australia's largest high-grade major gold deposit. Historically, it is Australia's largest high-grade gold producer of 6,600,000 ounces of gold ore averaging 38g/t (nearly 2 ounces per tonne of ore).

The historical mines were very profitable paying an estimated one billion dollars (in today's dollars) in dividends to their shareholders.

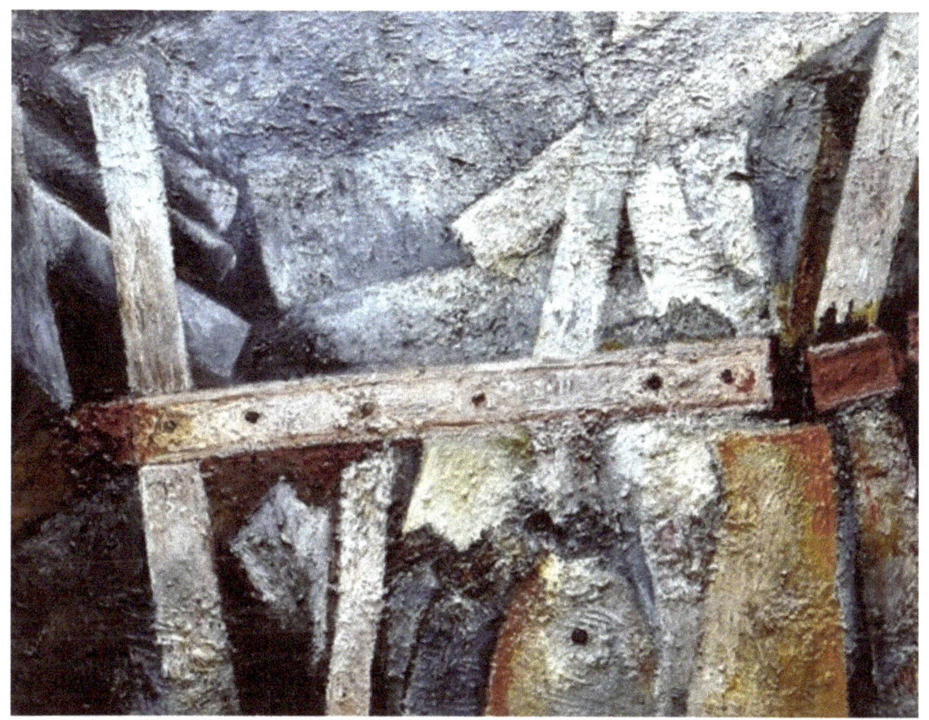

"Old Workings"

Medium: Gouache on paper

The "Old Workings" on the Charters Towers goldfield was painted in the open air.

Painting away from the home in the open air is called "plein air" painting. It's a powerful and rewarding experience as you deal with the ever-changing and ephemeral qualities of light. Spontaneity and freshness are other advantages of painting in the open air.

When Alex Barlow and I visited Charters Towers, I made 10 gouache paintings. At the time we were staying in an old Queenslander backpackers' hostel.

It was January and the heat was excessive. The road outside was so hot you could have fried an egg on the bitumen.

Trying to paint during the day was impossible. Because of the extreme heat, I had to paint just after sunrise so early in the morning we would leave the backpackers and go on to the goldfield.

Given it was an uncomfortable painting experience I had to paint fast so that I could return to the backpackers to escape the heat.

I exhibited these gouache paintings at a very successful solo show in Canberra.

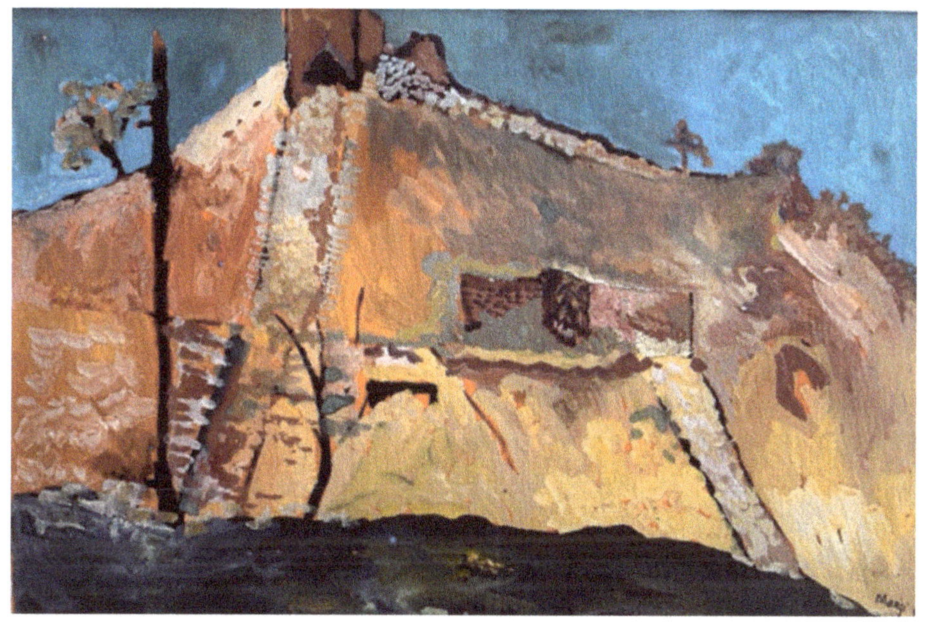

Chapter 3

Chinese in Australia

"The Pigtail"

Medium: Gouache sketch on paper

In the 1850s Chinese men started arriving in Australia to work on the goldfields. From the European perspective, it seemed as though the Chinese were arriving at an alarming rate. By mid-1855 around 17,000 Chinese were on the goldfields and by 1861, nearly 40,000 had arrived.

Given the flood of Chinese onto the goldfields it was not long before resentment and ill-feeling grew. There were various reasons for the growth of this anti-Chinese sentiment.

For one thing, the Chinese looked very different to the Europeans. The men had pigtails. They wore strange, conical-shaped hats and long garments which resembled women's clothing or else they wore blue padded jackets, wide pantaloons, and white socks.

The Chinese on the goldfields is the theme in one of my books that I published in 2022 *Gold and the Chinese: Racism, Riots and Protest on the Australian Goldfields*. The Chinese question was a subject of hot debate both on the goldfields and beyond. The response by the colonial government was to implement poll taxes and restrictions to limit the number of Chinese entering Australia.

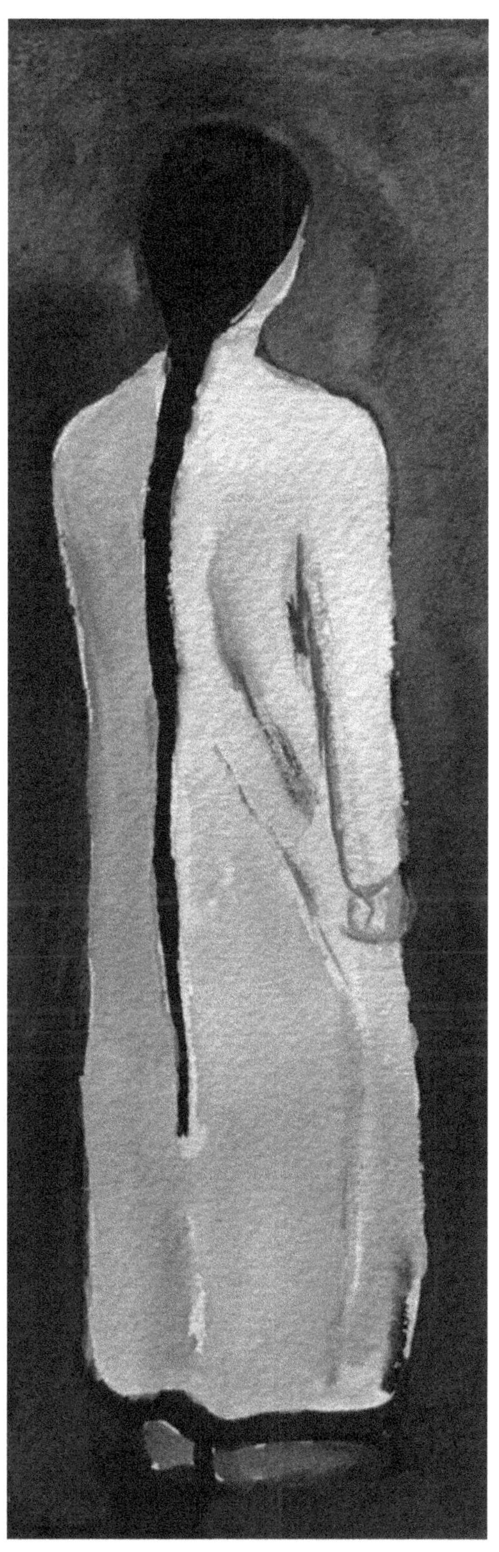

"Chinese Man Carrying His Load"
Medium: Gouache sketch on paper

Many Chinese immigrants arrived at Robe in South Australia. They travelled in large parties to the goldfields as this gave them better protection from bushrangers.

They would walk in single file in groups of up to 700 carrying their belongings in baskets hanging from bamboo poles.

Loads would hang from bamboo poles carried across their shoulders. The bamboo pole was balanced with an evenly distributed load suspended at each end - a typical sight.

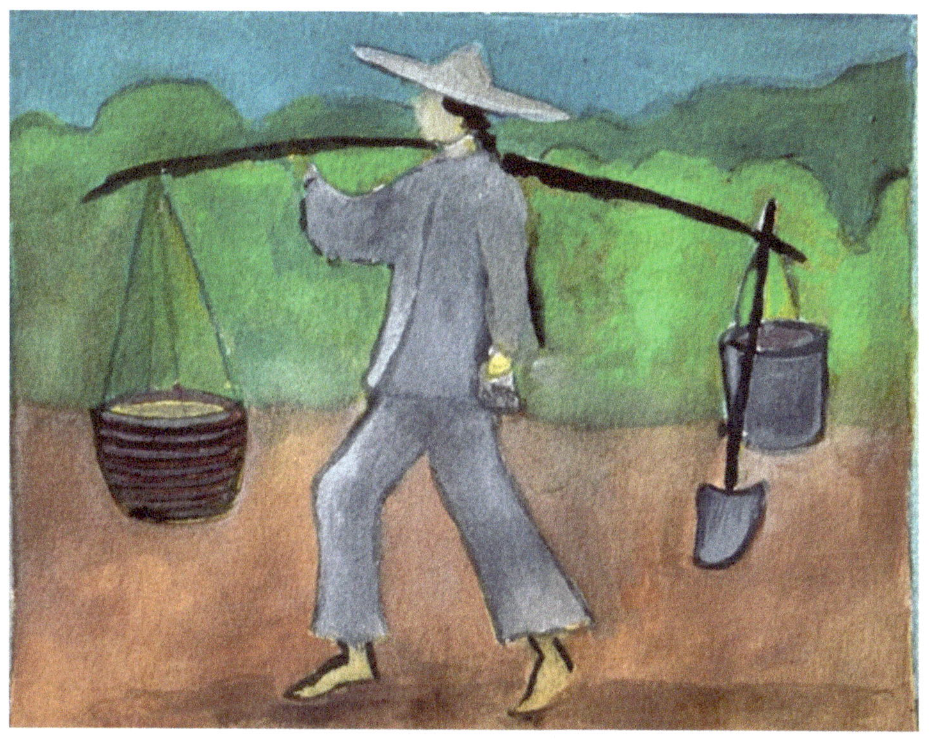

"Chinese Temple"

Medium: Gouache on paper

The "Chinese Temple," an illustration based on the Bendigo Joss House Temple, is one of the images in my book *Gold and the Chinese.*

Rumours circulated about the Chinese on the goldfields – the smoking of opium, gambling and getting women for prostitution. These stories led to ill feeling towards the Chinese; they became hated, and this eventually led to anti-Chinese sentiment and aggression.

In 1857 there was a riot in the Buckland Valley in Victoria when tensions between at least 2,000 Chinese and hundreds of European miners erupted. A newly constructed temple there was torched and burnt to ashes.

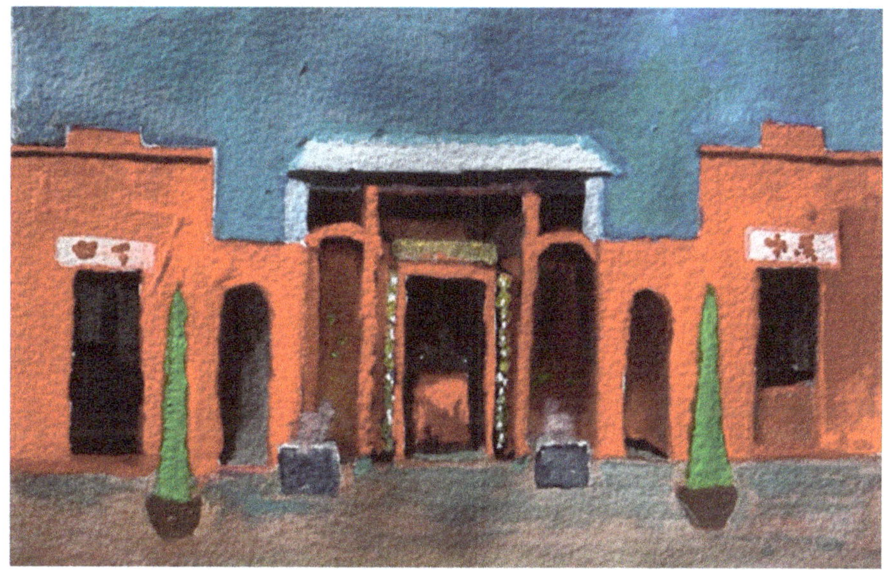

Chapter 4

Landscape

"Springbrook Kookaburra"

Medium: Gouache on paper

The inspiration for "Springbrook Kookaburra" came from an art excursion to the Springbrook National Park in southeast Queensland.

The Springbrook National Park is part of the Gondwana Rainforests of Australia World Heritage Area. If you look west from Queensland's Gold Coast coastal strip, you'll see the hinterland's mountain range that is the backdrop to the golden beaches.

I decided that Purling Brook Picnic Ground at Springbrook was a suitable place to paint.

I surveyed the surrounding rainforest and identified a couple of spots that looked worthwhile subjects and I had the companionship of an inquisitive brush turkey, a friendly kookaburra, a seasonally cranky magpie, and a crow lookalike, the currawong.

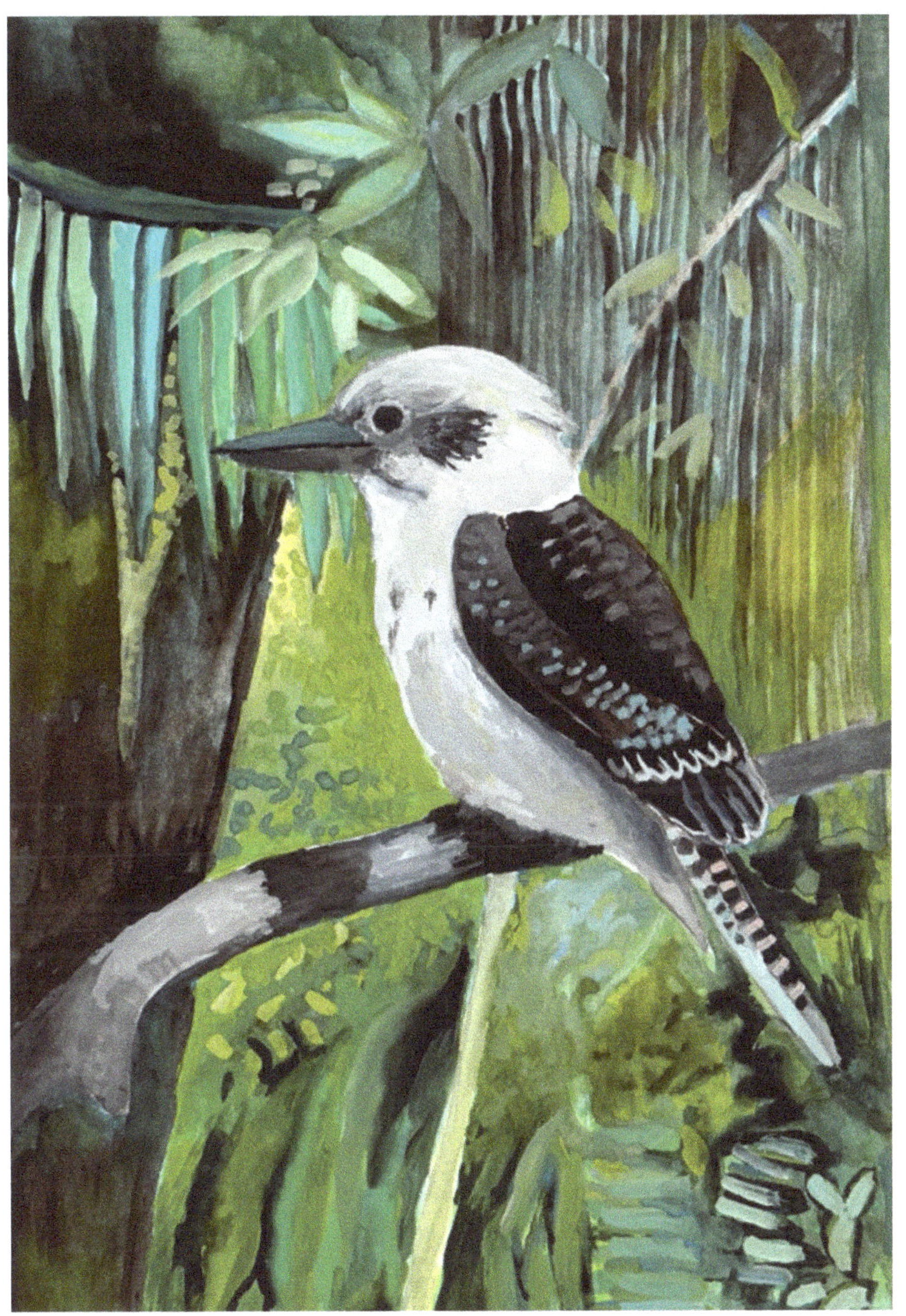

"Link Back to a Past Millennia"

Medium: Gouache on paper

Rainforests covered most of the Gondwana Rainforests of the Australian World Heritage Area. Still today, these rainforests with their plants and animals are a living link not only to Australia's past but to their future evolution.

The lush rainforests which incorporate the Springbrook National Park connect you to a world of great antiquity.

It is home to a unique ecological and magical environment of ancient fern families, cycad and conifer species, diverse tree species and animals like the Chelidae turtles, leaf-tailed geckoes and angle-headed dragons.

These species connect back to the days of the dinosaurs in the past millennia.

In the Springbrook National Park that I talk about in my book *Inspired by Country: An Artist's Journey Back to Nature: Landscape Painting with Gouache* are spectacular waterfalls, ancient trees, impressive views, and a unique world of natural beauty.

You absorb the crystal clean, fresh mountain air and this is an experience that takes you back in time to those early days of evolution.

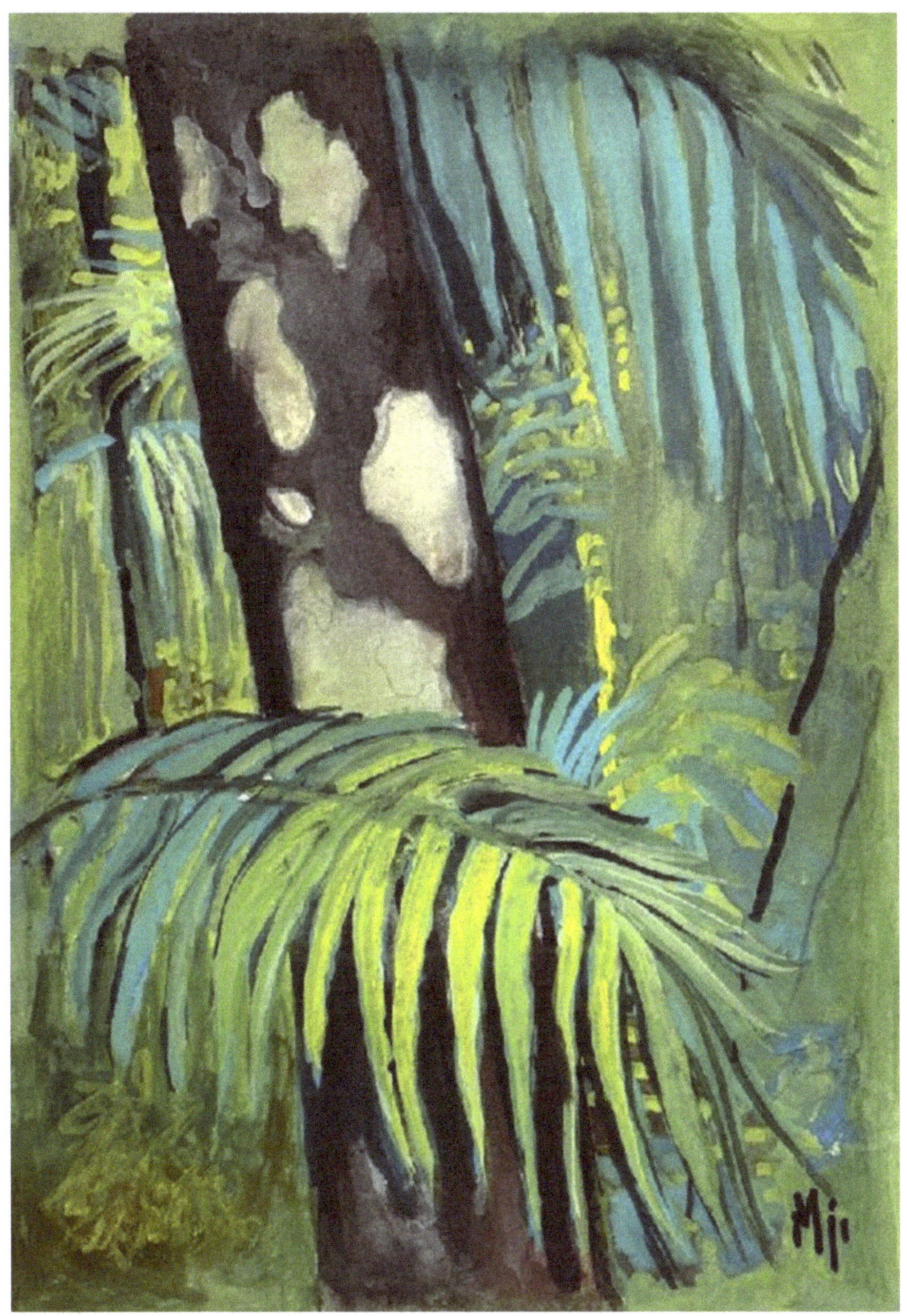

"Natural Bridge"

Medium: Gouache on paper

Natural Bridge, also known as Natural Arch, lies at the base of Springbrook in the Gold Coast hinterland. It is accessed from Numinbah Valley along the road to Murwillumbah.

Its rock pool and cave were contoured by an ongoing process of erosion. Rainfall fed the streams and waterfalls and the power of swirling waters over millions of years carved away volcanic rock and broke through into the cave below.

I remember as a child visiting this cave and being dared by my brother to plunge into the cold rock pool. Ever since and from time to time I make the pilgrimage to Natural Bridge.

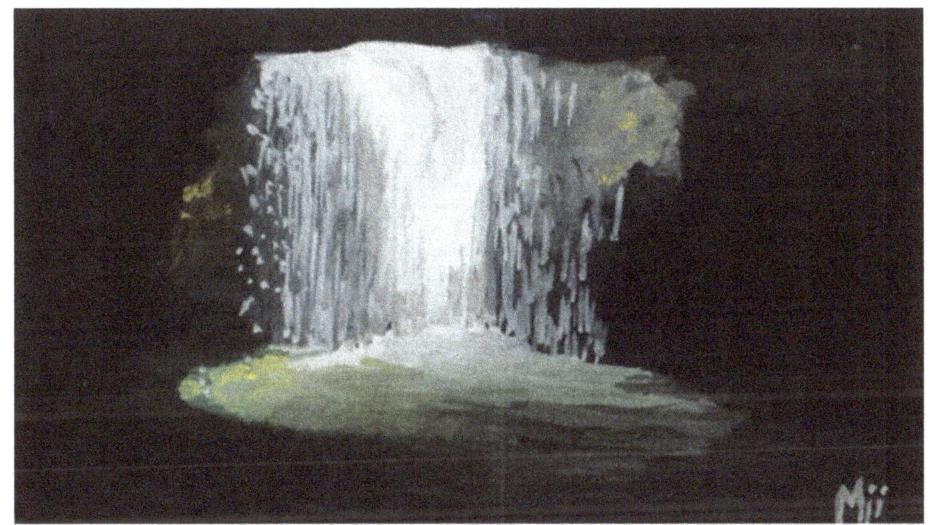

"Sculptured Contours"

Medium: Gouache on paper

The landscape you see from the Springbrook National Park was shaped by molten lava from the massive Tweed volcano which was active some 23 million years ago. About 10 million years ago the volcano began to die.

Volcanic activity extending from Springbrook to the Lamington plateau and the Tweed Range sculptured the landscape. In the process, the magnificent, classic erosion caldera landform of Wollumbin (commonly known as Mount Warning) was created. This deeply sacred mountain was the volcano's epicentre.

Whether you view the countryside from Springbrook, from Byron Bay, from the highway in the Northern Rivers, the haunting Wollumbin dominates the region.

It is a constant reminder of that ancient world when lava spilt in every direction for up to 100 kilometres. When it cooled it became the rocks and high plateau areas typical of the area.

This Tweed volcano is regarded as possibly the best-preserved erosion caldera in the world.

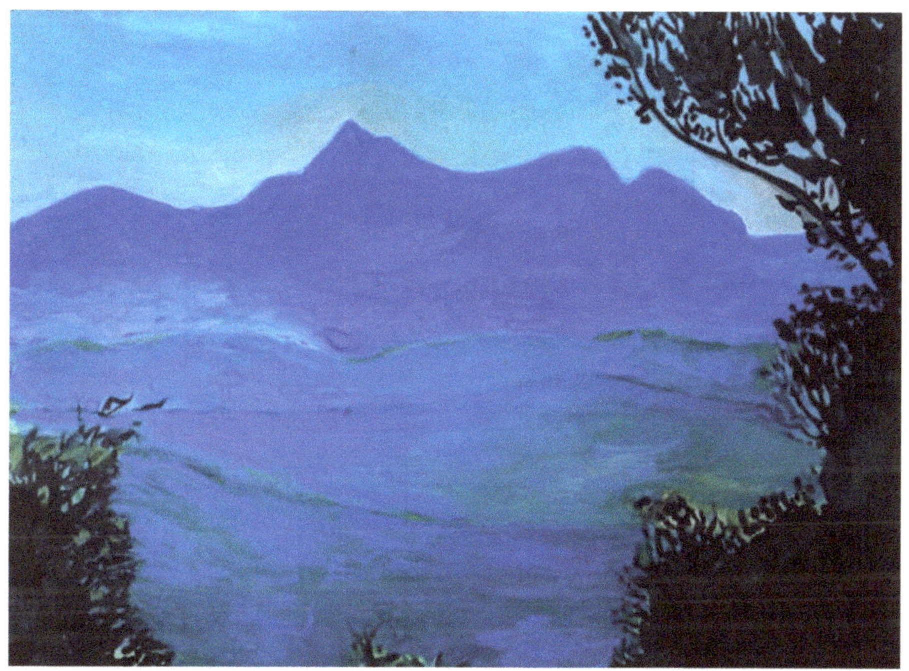

"Tulip Farm"

Medium: Gouache on paper

Every year in Canberra there is a spectacular garden experience, the Floriad.

When the Floriad festival is on, you can take a short drive to Sutton, New South Wales, just outside the Australian Capital Territory (ACT). It is four hectares of blooms and blossoms at the Tulip Top Gardens.

In conjunction with Floriad, the gardens are open to the public. There you can view and experience the magic of over fifty varieties of tulips.

With its explosion of colour, the tulip farm for me was an inspirational setting. I visited it many times and created artwork based on its mesmerising floral sensations.

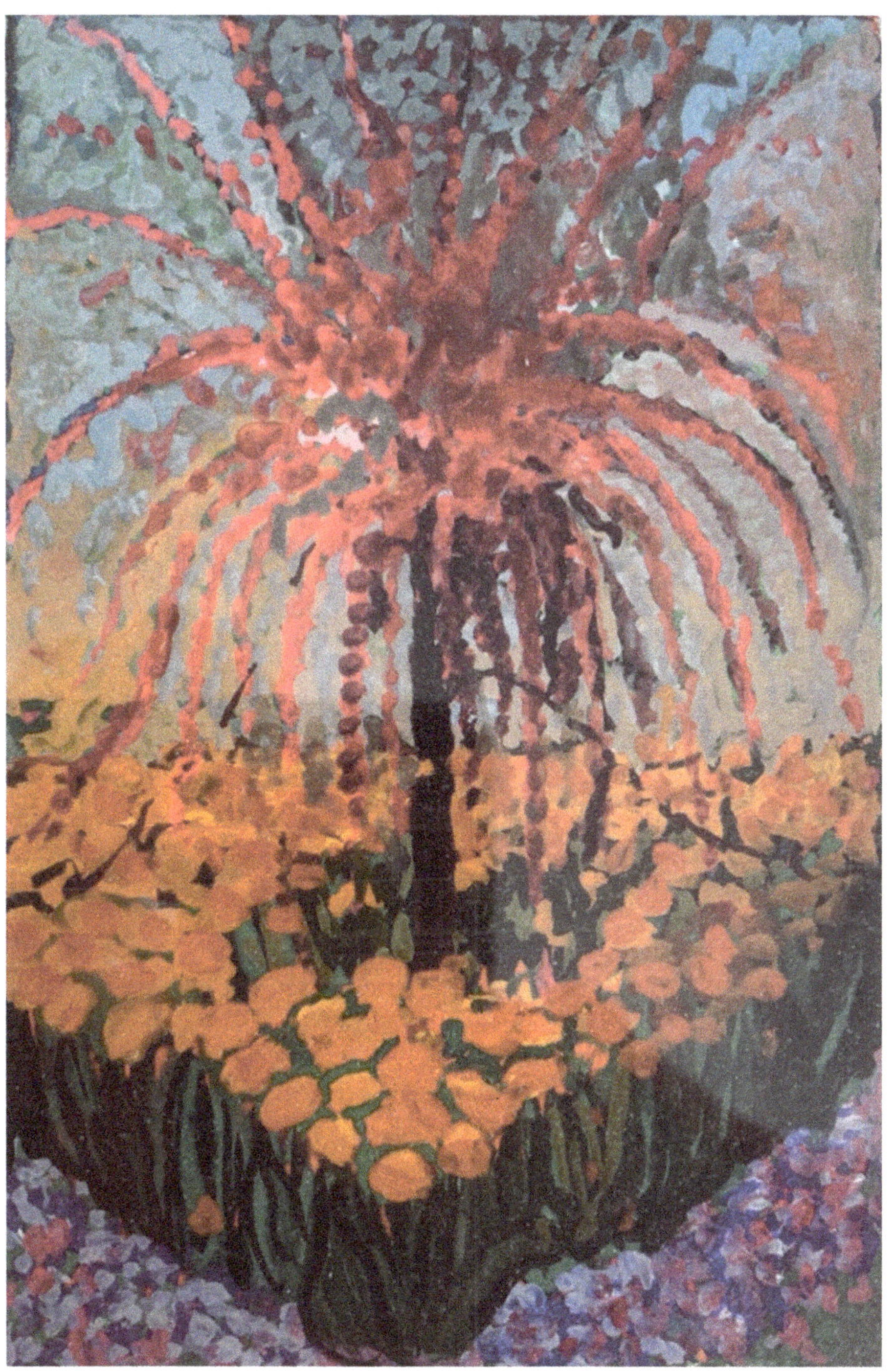

"Lake Crackenback"

Medium: Oil on canvas

When we lived in Canberra, Alex Barlow and I loved to escape for a few days of rest and recreation. We visited the Snowy Mountains in summertime and enjoyed the magic of alpine Australia taking in the incredible views and mountain atmosphere.

Our favourite places to stay were Thredbo, Lake Eucumbene, Charlottes Pass, and Lake Crackenback. One of the highlights of these trips was our hike from Charlottes Pass to the summit of Mount Kosciuszko.

At Charlottes Pass, I painted in the open air which inadvertently generated much curiosity and interest for the visiting tourists.

On one of our excursions to the Snowy Mountains, we stayed at the Lake Crackenback Resort and Spa. I remember the crisp, cold mountain air, snuggling up under the doona enjoying a siesta, and absorbing the views over the lake bordered by the Kosciuszko National Park and the majestic Thredbo River.

As I soaked up the experience, I made sketches and eventually back at home in Canberra I created this heavily textured, semi-abstract oil.

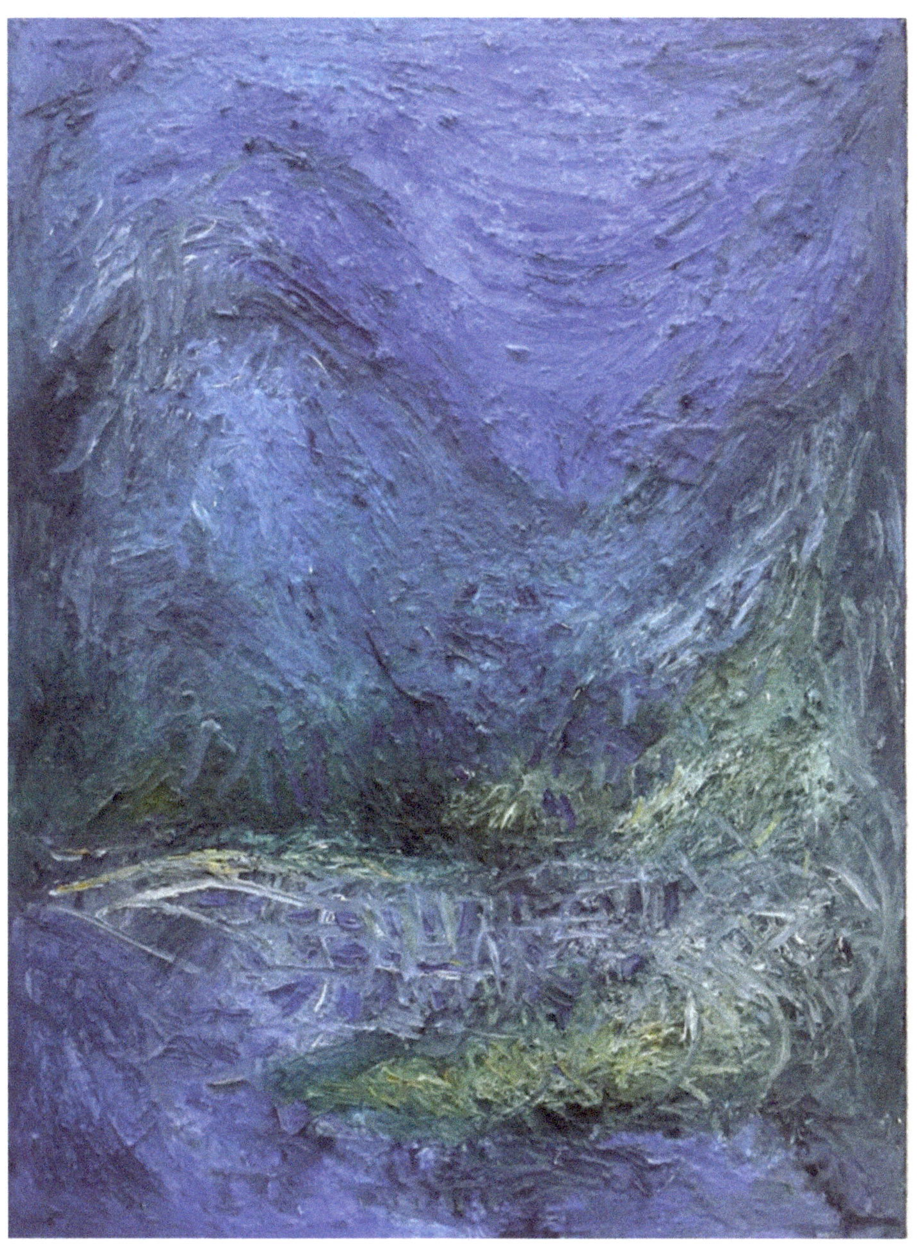

"Moruya Moon"

Collection: Surfers Paradise Catholic Parish
Medium: Oil on canvas

The south coast of New South Wales was another region Alex and I visited. We would chill out in the cabins on the shores of Wallaga Lake or at cabins near Narooma.

Once we drove from Narooma to Moruya in the evening. There had been a lot of fires and some of the tree trunks were still burning.

Along the way, we had an eerie experience. We came across a dead horse in the middle of the road. This was a mystery, and we never had any explanation as to how it ended up there.

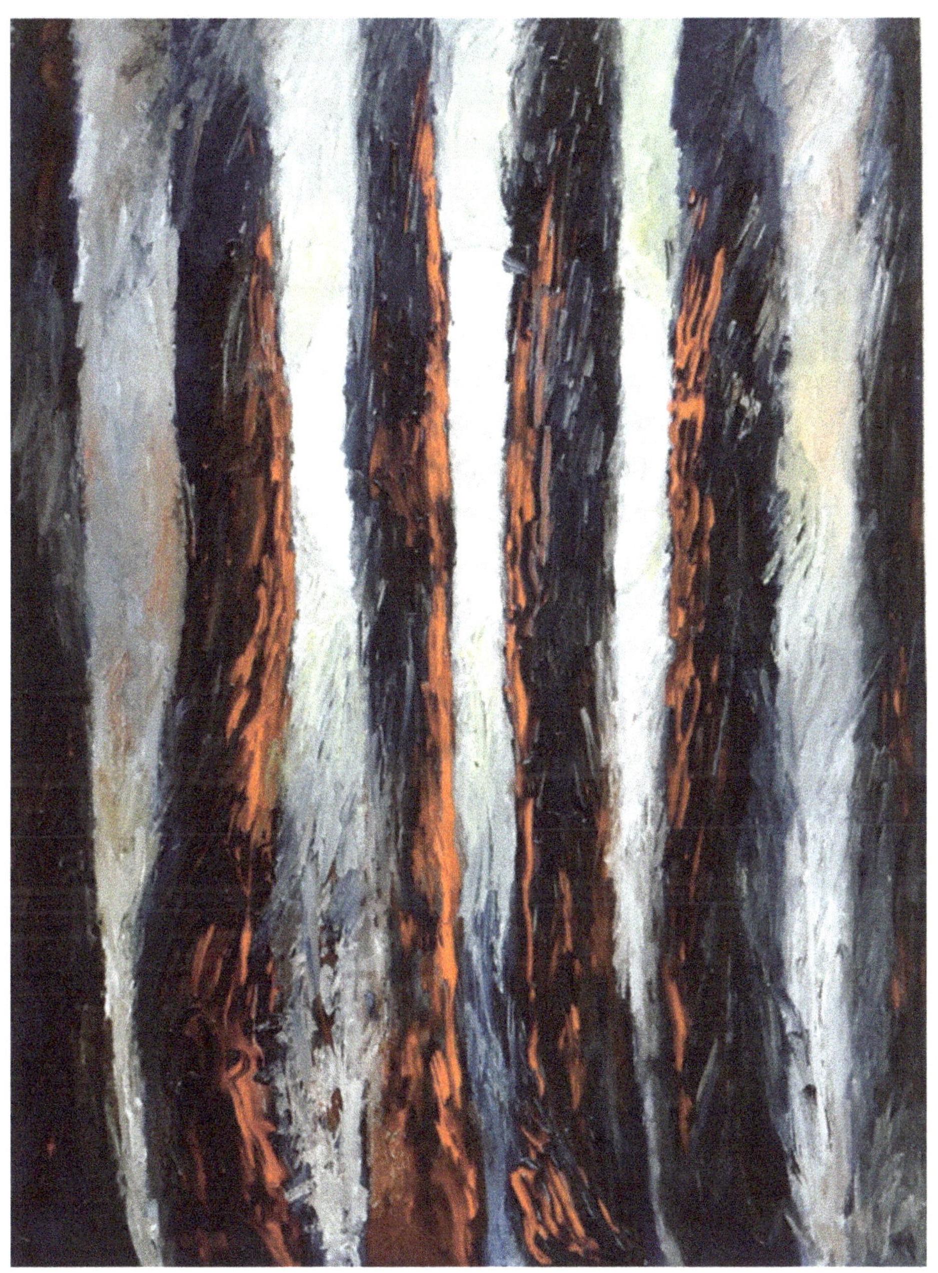

"Monaro Hills"

Collection: Surfers Paradise Catholic Parish
Medium: Oil on canvas

I said earlier that we loved to take time out to enjoy the magic of alpine Australia or to drive to the south coast to places like Wallaga Lake.

As we drove out from the Australian Capital Territory, we regularly took the Monaro Highway and headed towards Cooma.

The rolling hills in the Monaro region with its amazing vistas were remarkable and I was inspired to make this heavily textured oil painting.

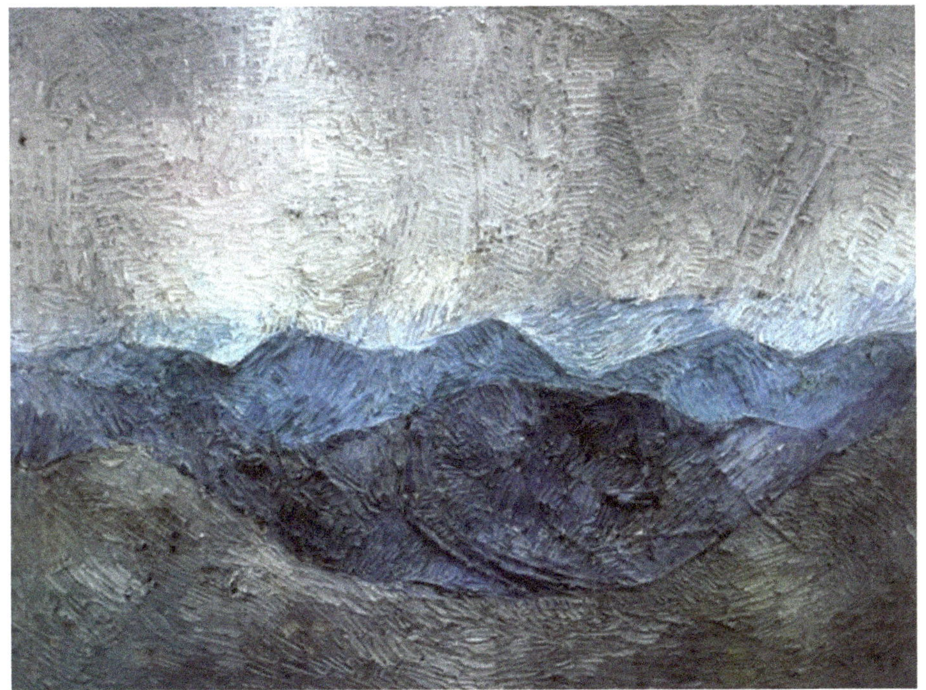

"Hinze Dam"

Medium: Gouache on paper

Alex and I lived in Canberra for 30 years but from time to time we visited the Gold Coast in Queensland when we attended the annual Pro-Ma Systems Convention.

By 2006 our Canberra chapter was at an end. We spent a few years at Mosman Bay in Sydney. Then in 2011 we took the plunge and returned to the state of our birth – Queensland.

Alex was born in Brisbane, and I in Surfers Paradise. For me, it was a return to my roots as I always loved the Gold Coast and its hinterland.

Just outside the Gold Coast on the road to Numinbah Valley is the Hinze Dam. It's a favourite stopping place for people exploring the region. While you take in the stunning vistas you experience the delights of the View Café with its phenomenal views over the 310 giga-litre dam.

Like the Springbrook National Park 23 million years ago this area was part of the massive volcano Wollumbin (Mt Warning). The crater rim is 2 kilometres tall with lava flows that sprawl across more than 7,000 square kilometres. The caldera of this shield volcano currently has a diameter of over 40kms making it the largest erosion caldera in the southern hemisphere.

The Hinze Dam was built on the Nerang River in 1976 and was expanded in 1989 and again in 2011. It is positioned within this geological marvel and is surrounded by Mount Tamborine, Springbrook, Beechmont and Binna Burra.

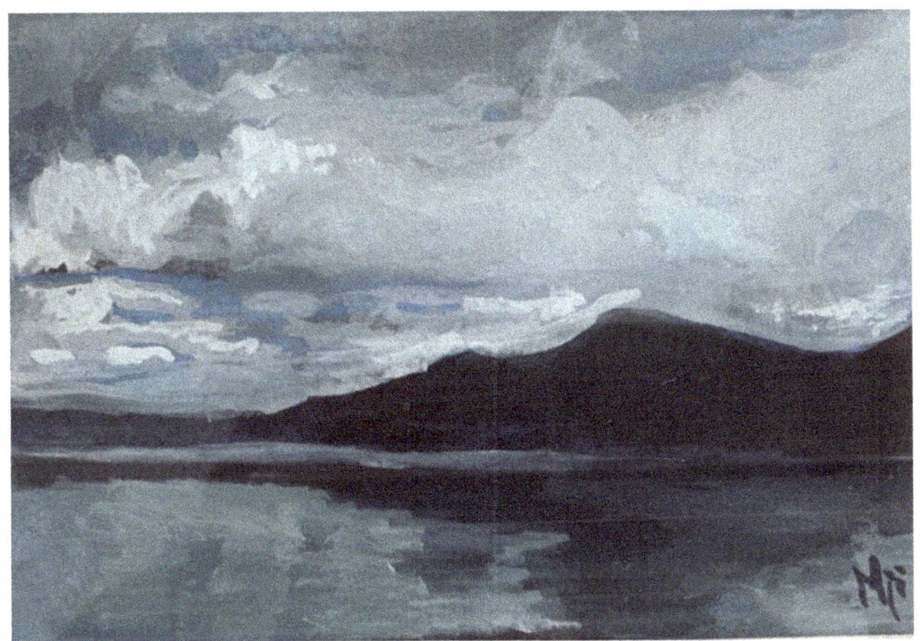

"Beechmont at Dawn"

Medium: Gouache on paper

A favourite retreat of mine in the Gold Coast region are the Wantalanya Chalets at Beechmont.

The chalets are located on the Beechmont Plateau only minutes away from Binna Burra and the Lamington National Park.

I love these rustic self-contained cabins with amazing views across the Numinbah Valley to the Gold Coast. I've made many memorable visits there usually to have a weekend of painting or to finalise the next book.

This magnetic setting is the perfect sanctuary for stimulating the creative juices. I love to wake up early and watch the spellbinding dawn break over the Gold Coast skyline.

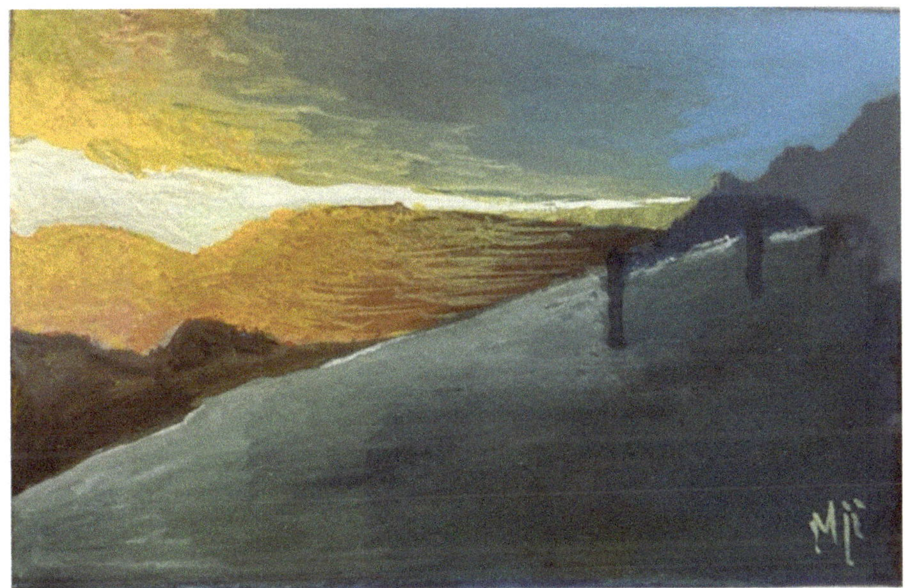

"Yarramalong Park"

Medium: Gouache on paper

Yarramalong Park at Aratula, a few kilometres from Boonah, is a 65-hectare (160 acre) property nestled in the beautiful Scenic Rim. This private thoroughbred stud owned by Richard and Joanie Foster is the breeding ground for many champions.

In addition to the horse stud is an exclusive and secluded bush campground nestled at the base of Little Mt Edwards.

As you drive into the property there is an old, historic bank – the original Commercial Bank which came from Mt Alford (10 minutes from Boonah). Its backdrop is Mt Edwards rising 634 metres (2,080 ft) above sea level and part of the Moogerah Peaks National Park.

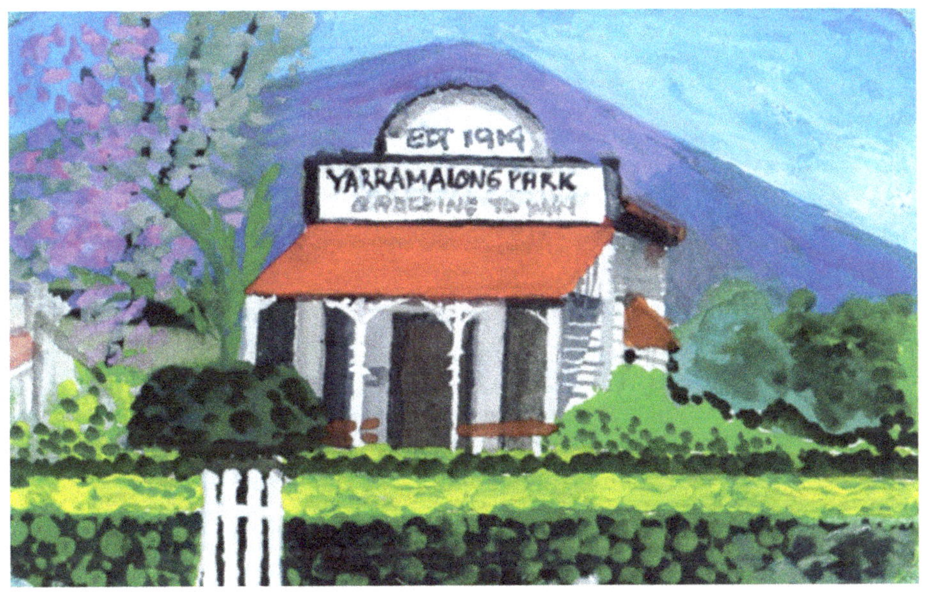
EST 1914
YARRAMALONG PARK
BREEDING TO WIN

"Couran Cove"

Collection: Branko Sola
Medium: Gouache on paper

Situated on South Stradbroke Island, Couran Cove is a 30-minute ferry ride from Marina Mirage at Main Beach on the Gold Coast.

It's a natural paradise where you wake up each morning to the rising sun over the billabong. There are pristine beaches, secluded rainforests, and calm waters. You hear the call of native birds and the hushed roll of distant surf. It's a sanctuary for the wallabies who make their presence felt amongst the visiting tourists.

Couran Cove is the perfect island escape and has been an inspirational source for some of my artwork.

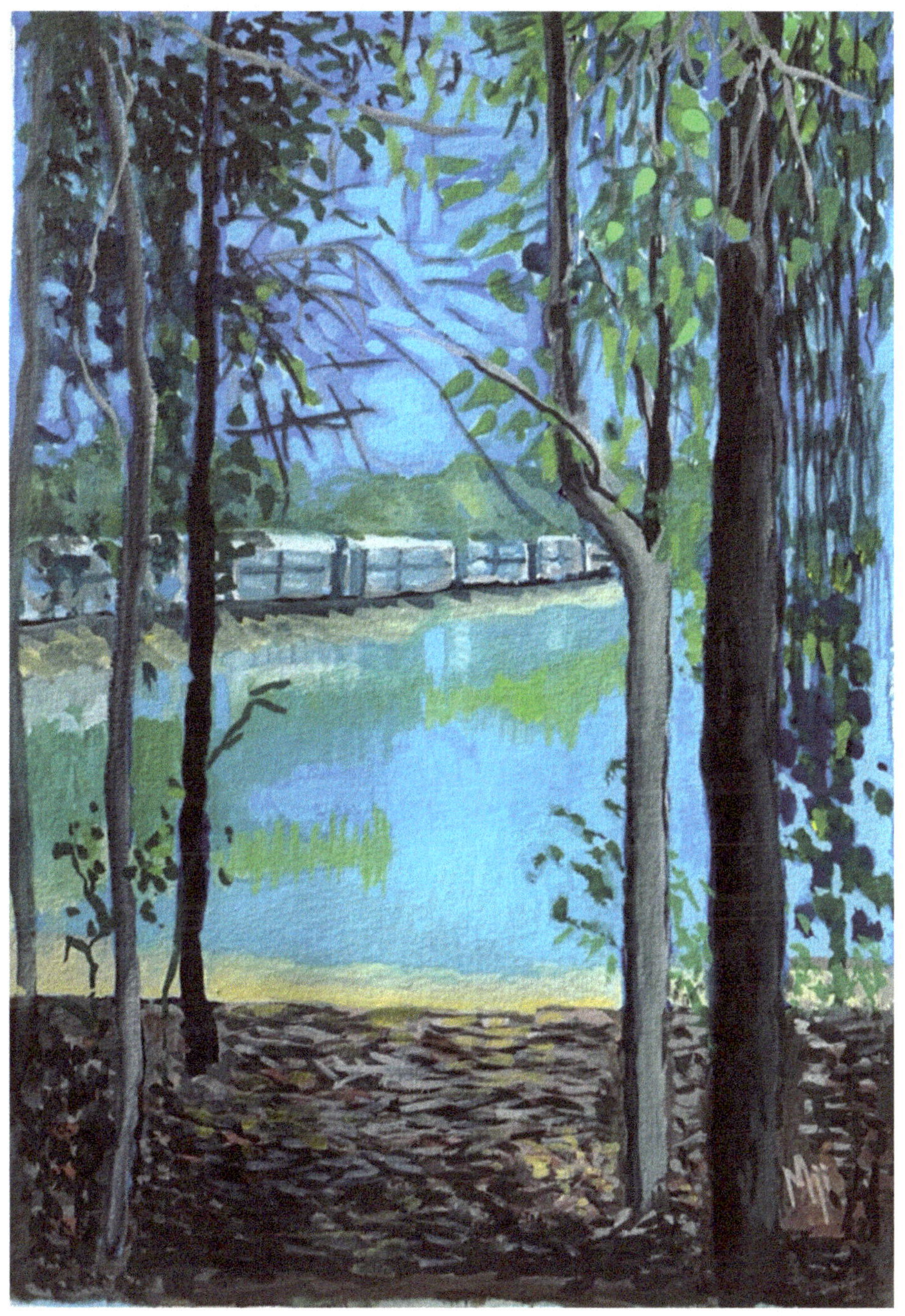

"Tree Roots, Couran Cove"

Collection: Branko Sola
Medium: Gouache on paper

Couran Cove boasts a mangrove swamp, a rainforest, wetlands, eucalypt woodlands and coastal dunes.

When staying at Couran Cove, I take an early morning stroll on the boardwalk through the deafening silence of the secluded rainforest. I am treated to its many wonders as I step into what seems like a magical storybook.

I come across the gnarled roots of a tree, a symbol of resilience and strength, which teaches us about staying grounded through times of difficulty and stress.

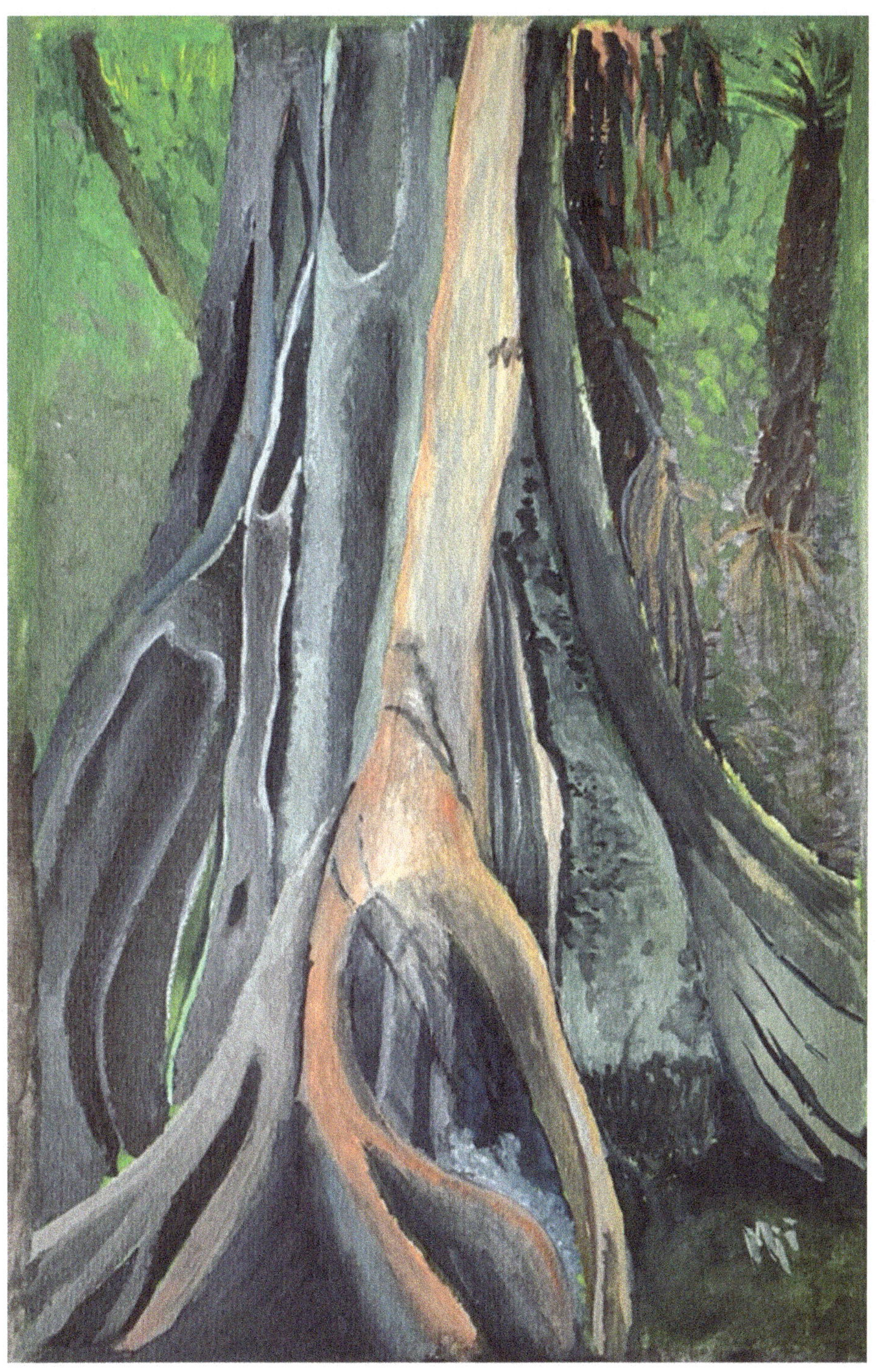

"Secluded Rainforest"

Collection: Branko Sola
Medium: Gouache on paper

Many natural highlights of the Gold Coast can only be appreciated and accessed on foot and at Couran Cove the eco-adventure continues.

Enjoy the calming influence of the rainforest.

Numerous studies show that both exercising in a forest or simply looking at trees can reduce blood pressure as well as the stress-related hormones cortisol and adrenaline.

A walk in the forest impacts the body and mind; it stimulates the senses, and you can't but help notice the smells of the forest, the sunlight falling on rocks, and the soft moss, and ferns on the forest floor.

Plein air painting equally has health benefits. It's a meditative experience, another way of practising mindfulness and being in the present. There is something special about painting trees, the artist is drawn to their symbolism of life, growth, renewal, and rebirth.

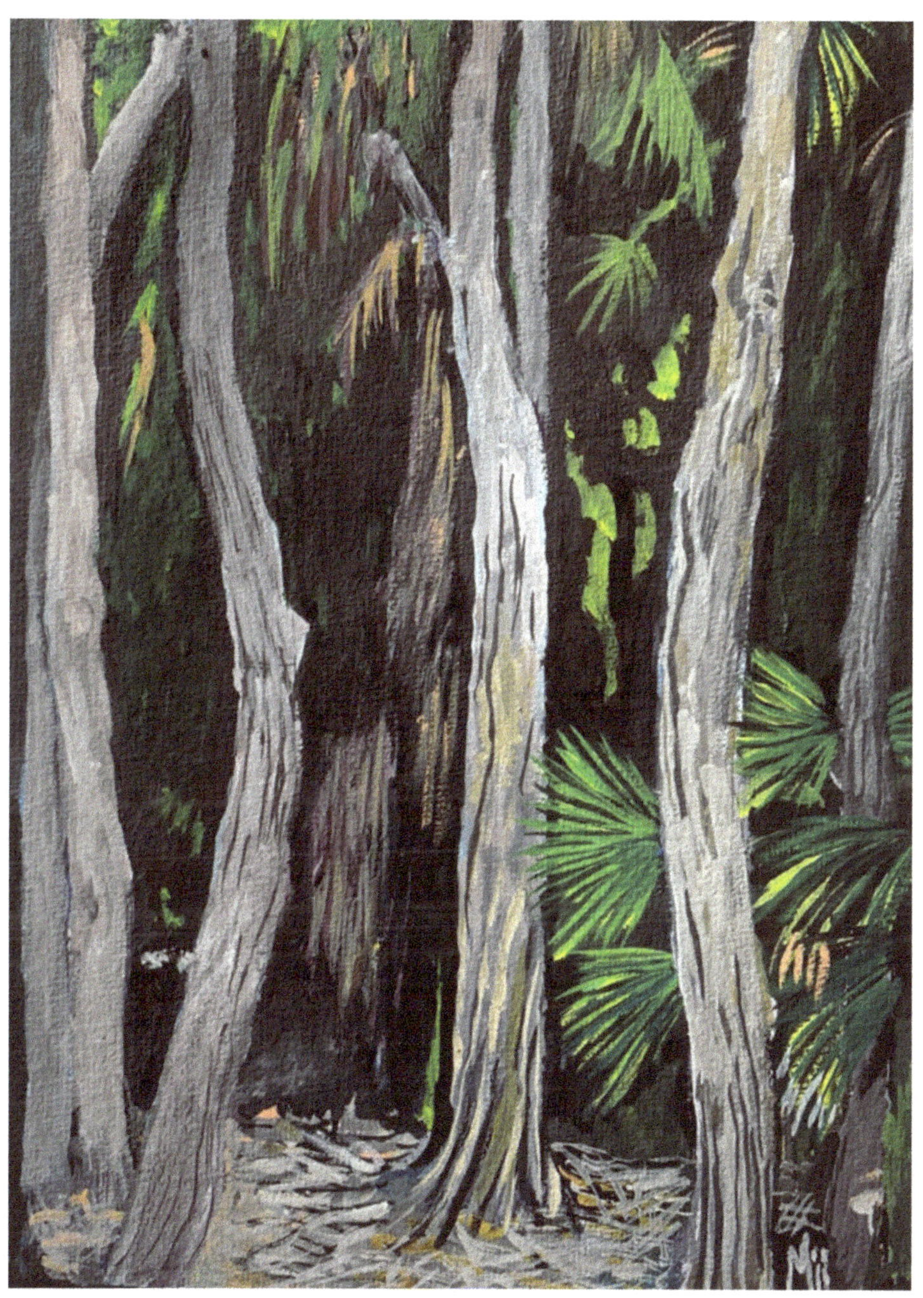

Chapter 5

First Nations

"Punitive Expedition"

Collection: Hill Family
Medium: Oil on Canvas

1988 saw the publication of *Six Australian Battlefields*. As a result of researching and writing this book I made a lot of paintings many of which were exhibited at solo shows in Sydney, Canberra, and Melbourne.

In 1976 along with my partner, Alex Barlow, I was a Research Fellow in Education at the Australian Institute of Aboriginal and Torres Strait Islander Studies (AIATSIS). At the same time, I was enrolled at the Australian National University (ANU) doing my master's degree in Anthropology. I specialised in Aboriginal Studies and the focus of my studies was to uncover the hidden history of this country.

Part of the *Six Australian Battlefields* series of paintings was "Punitive Expedition." This is a large, very textured oil painting 152.4 x 182.88cm.

It was inspired by the patrols by the Queensland Native Police who had to protect the pastoralists, miners, and colonialists on the frontier. Their method of "protection" was to kill, and the victims were First Nations people who were in turn trying to protect their land, lives and loved ones.

The recruiting method was to select First Nations men who lived in far distant places. The idea was to try to avoid conflict between First Nations groups, so the strategy was to recruit First Nations police from other groups that were a long way away.

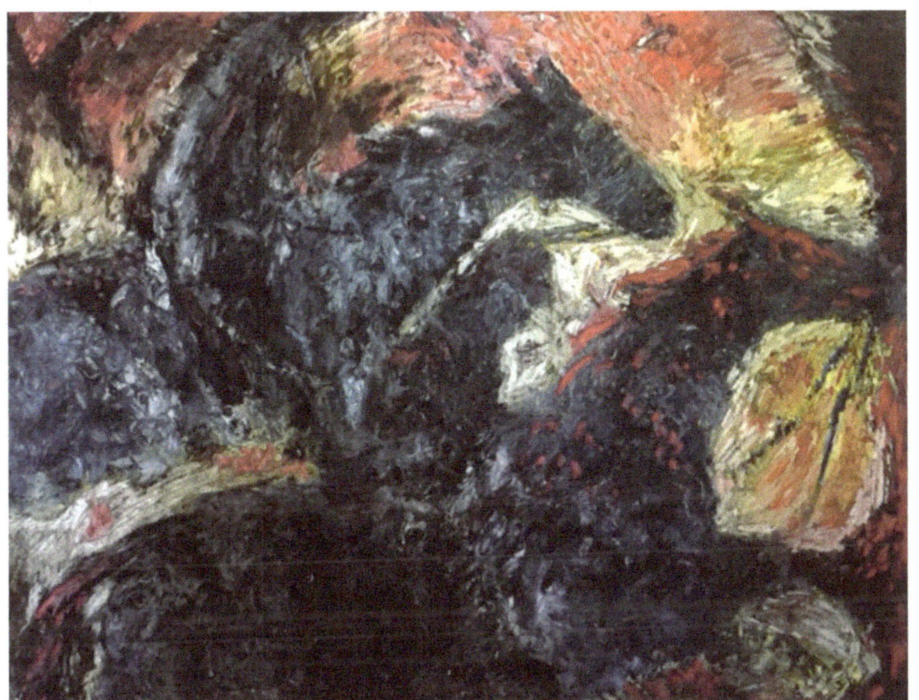

"Tent Embassy"

Medium: Gouache on paper

In 1972 on the lawns of the old Parliament House in Canberra, four activists erected the Aboriginal Tent Embassy to protest against the treatment of First Nations people in Australia.

A beach umbrella was erected on Australia Day — 26 January 1972 — and a sign said Aboriginal Embassy. This was a political statement designed to highlight the fact that First Nations people were being treated like foreigners in their own country.

There were various attempts to remove the Tent Embassy, but it remained on the lawns of Parliament House until 1975. For many years the Embassy was set up at various locations around Canberra.

It became a symbol of injustice to First Nations people. In 1992 the Embassy was permanently re-established on its original site and it continues to this day to be a site of Aboriginal protest and a reminder of the issues that face First Nations Australians.

By this time the new Parliament House had moved to Capital Hill in Canberra, so the Tent Embassy was positioned on the lawns of the old Parliament House.

In 1995 it was listed on the Australian Heritage Council's National Estate.

This small painting is one of the illustrations in my book *First People Then and Now: Introducing Indigenous Australians.*

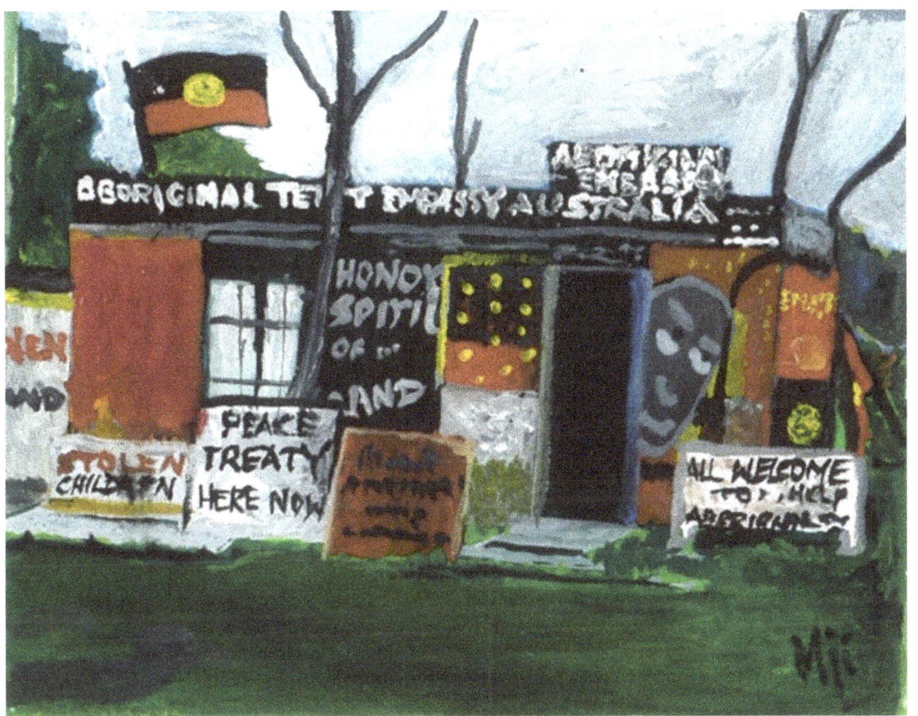
ABORIGINAL TENT EMBASSY AUSTRALIA
ABORIGINAL EMBASSY
HONO
SPITI
OF
AND
STOLEN
CHILDREN
PEACE
TREATY
HERE NOW
ALL WELCOME
TO HELP
ABORIGINALITY

"Yagan's Head"

Medium: Gouache on paper

Yagan (c.1795-1833) was a hero of First Nation resistance in the Swan River region of Western Australia.

He has become an iconic figure and symbol of the fight for Nyungar rights and recognition.

First Nations people fought wars of resistance against the British Empire. These started on the east coast of the Australian continent in 1788 a couple of years after the arrival of the First Fleet and spread to the west coast.

The First Nations people of southwest Western Australia are generally known as Nyungar (Nyoongar, Noongar). The Nyungar fiercely defended their rights and their lands.

The fate of Yagan in Western Australia in the early 1800s was death at the hands of the British. He was lured into an ambush, shot, his head severed, his entire skin cut off and the head smoked to preserve it.

Yagan's hair was combed, possum fur string was tied around the head as a headband and red and black cockatoo features were added.

The head was sent to England as a souvenir. The story of Yagan is in my book *Australian Aboriginal History: 5 Stories of Indigenous Heroes*.

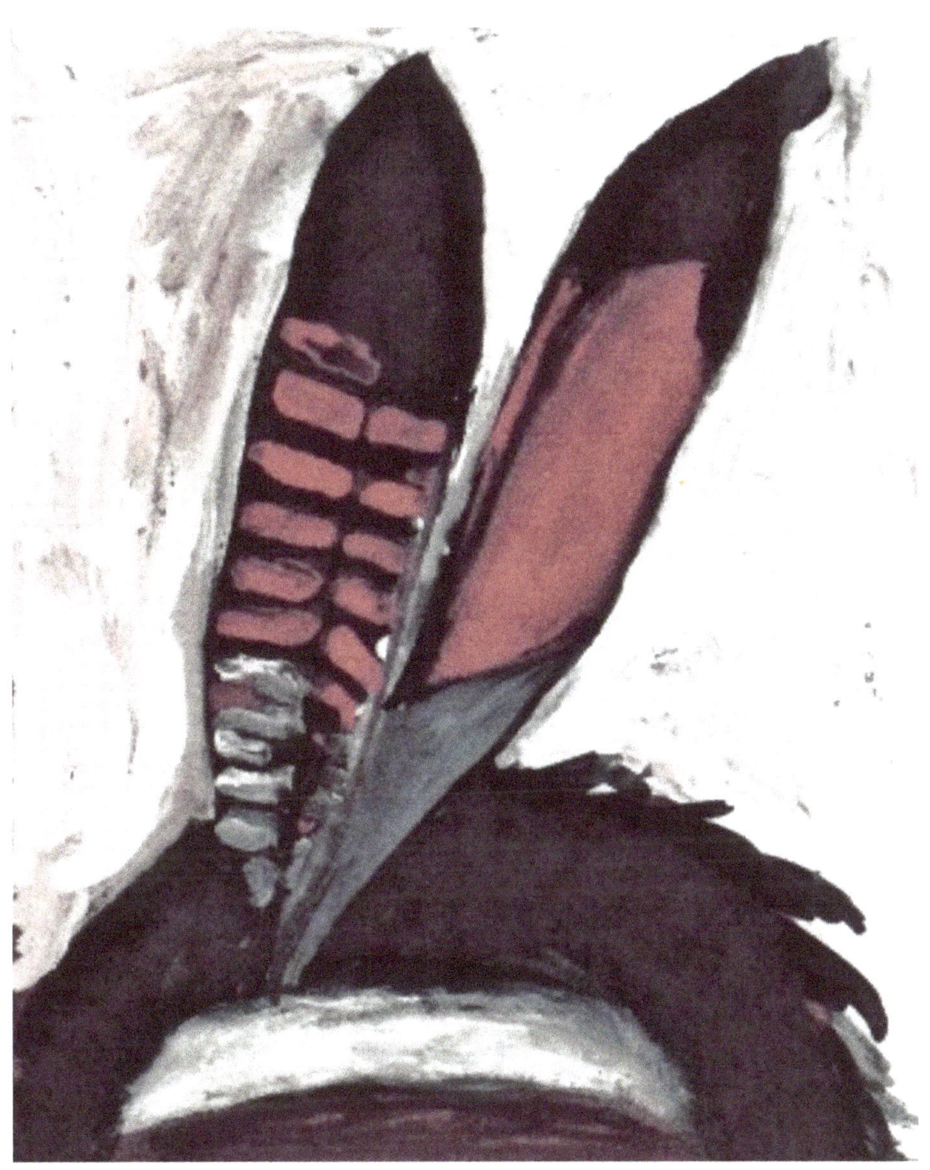

"Stolen Generation"

Medium: Oil on canvas

The Stolen Generations are the many First Nations people in Australia who were removed as children from their families and communities by government officials, church groups, and welfare bodies.

Children were taken and placed into institutions or fostered or adopted into white families. These First Nations children lost their land, their culture, their language, their songs, and their heritage. Subsequently, they felt they belonged neither to their Aboriginal heritage nor to white society.

These years of separation, sadness, and lost opportunity deeply scarred the psyches of many First Nation people.

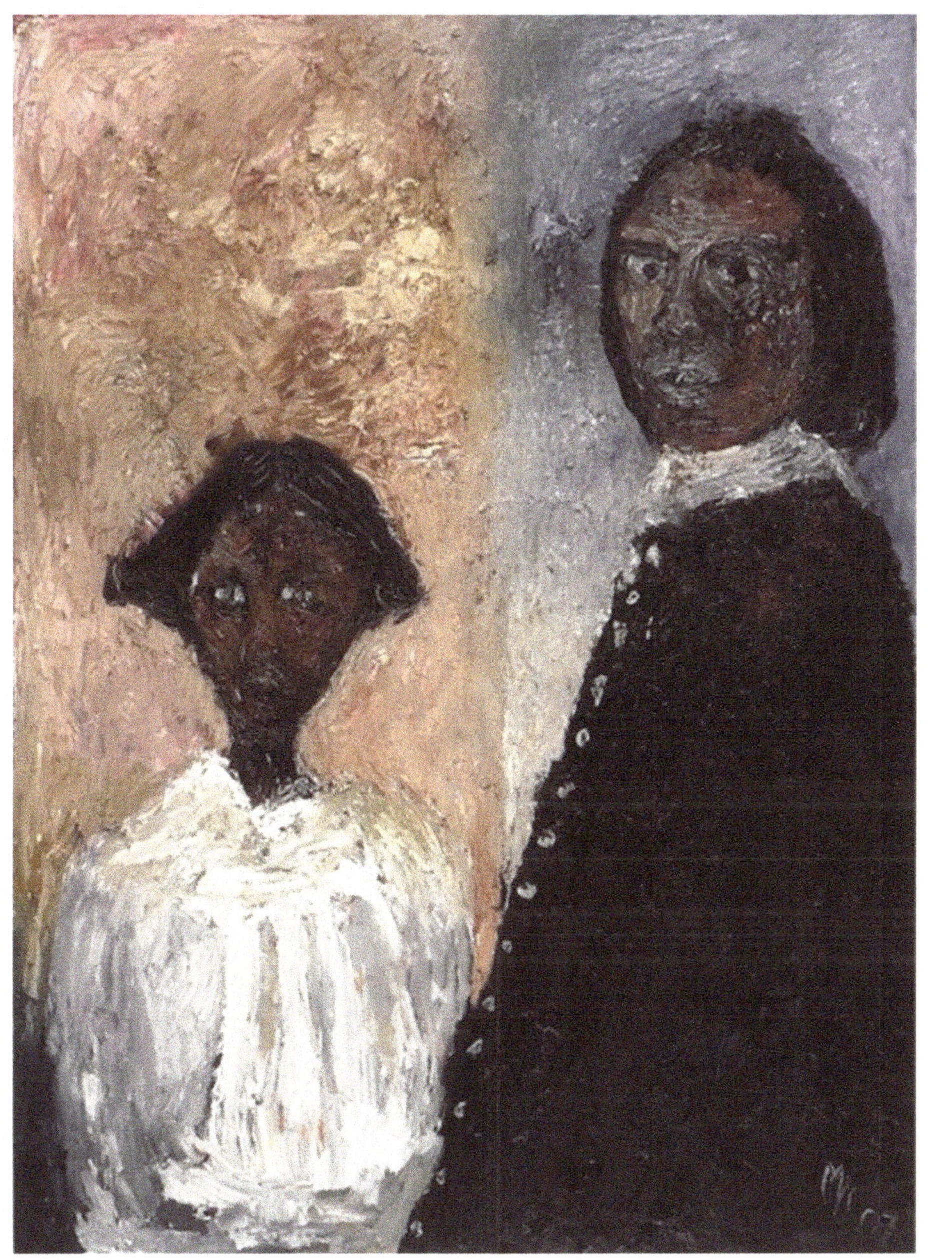

"The Servant"

Medium: Oil on canvas

When I was writing *The Apology: Saying Sorry to the Stolen Generations* I made a series of paintings on the Stolen Generations theme. This book published by Pearson is the story of the long journey towards reconciliation between Indigenous and non-Indigenous Australians, and the historic Apology made by Prime Minister Rudd to members of the Stolen Generations in Federal Parliament in 2008.

This painting "The Servant" is part of that series. With thick, textured oil paint I created this dark, forbidding painting trying to capture the emotional and psychological trauma experienced by members of the Stolen Generation.

The story of the Stolen Generations shows how important it is for a nation not only to take pride in past events but also to acknowledge the shameful chapters of its history.

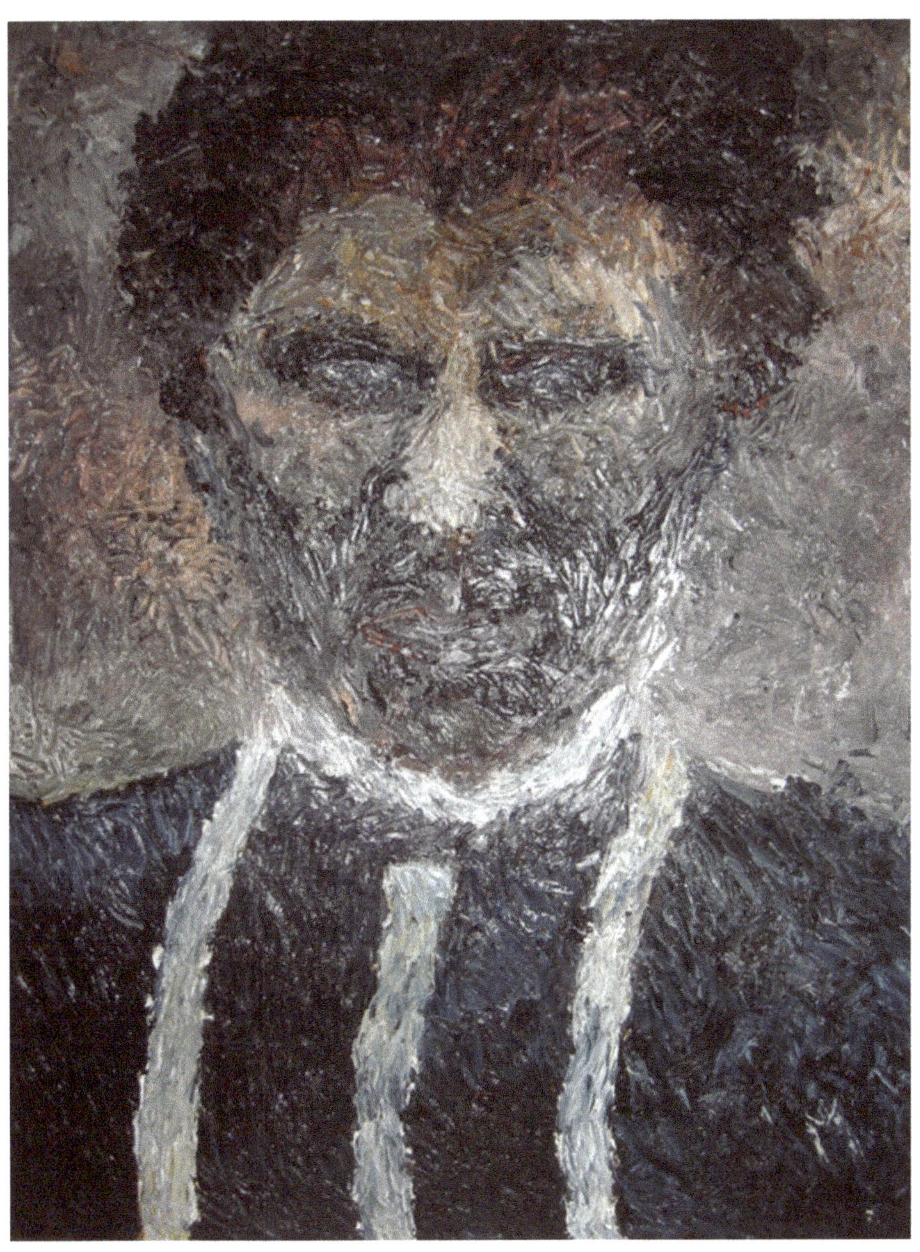

"Pemulwuy"

Medium: Gouache on paper

Pemulwuy (c.1760-1802) led the Eora resistance against British settlement which was continually expanding in the Sydney area and encroaching onto First Nations lands.

Pemulwuy emerged as a powerful guerrilla leader from the Botany Bay area of Sydney. Eventually, the British occupation force relegated his status to that of outlaw.

In 1802 Pemulwuy was shot by two settlers who had stalked him. His head was cut from his body, pickled, preserved in spirits, and sent to Sir Joseph Banks in England to add to his collection. Today the current whereabouts of the head are unknown.

Pemulwuy's assassination brought down a hero who had defied several governors in fierce resistance and who had won the admiration of both white and black. Above all, he contained for twelve years the cancer-like spread of the British invasion into Eora lands.

Like Yagan, you can find the Pemulwuy story in *Australian Aboriginal History: 5 Stories of Indigenous Heroes*.

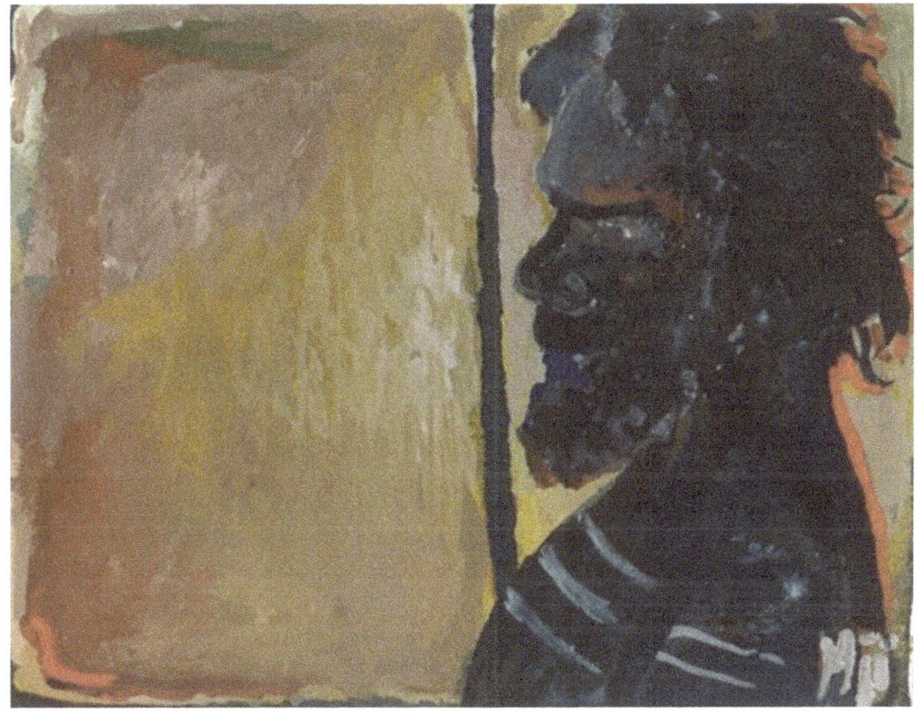

"Native Policeman"

Medium: Gouache on paper

Colonial governments had a policy of recruiting First Nations people into their police forces which was a tactic used throughout the British Empire for handling Indigenous resistance. This policy was designed to uphold British law and order.

As gold finds became commonplace in Australia, Native Police were used to guard new sites, patrol the goldfields, and provide law and order.

Lieutenant-Governor La Trobe in Victoria relied on his black-mounted police force to enforce the law on the goldfields. His Native Police were sent to patrol and support the gold commissioners on the goldfields and to inspect the mining licences.

In Queensland, Native Police had to protect the pastoralists, miners and colonialists on the frontier. They had to achieve this by whatever means were necessary. Their method of "protection" was to mount patrols and to kill.

The Queensland Native Police were the instrument of colonial policy bringing with it a reign of terror and violence.

My book *Blood Gold: Native Police, Bushrangers, and Law and Order on the Goldfields* explores how Native Police were used on Queensland's expanding frontier to "disperse" First Nation people from their lands to make way for colonisation.

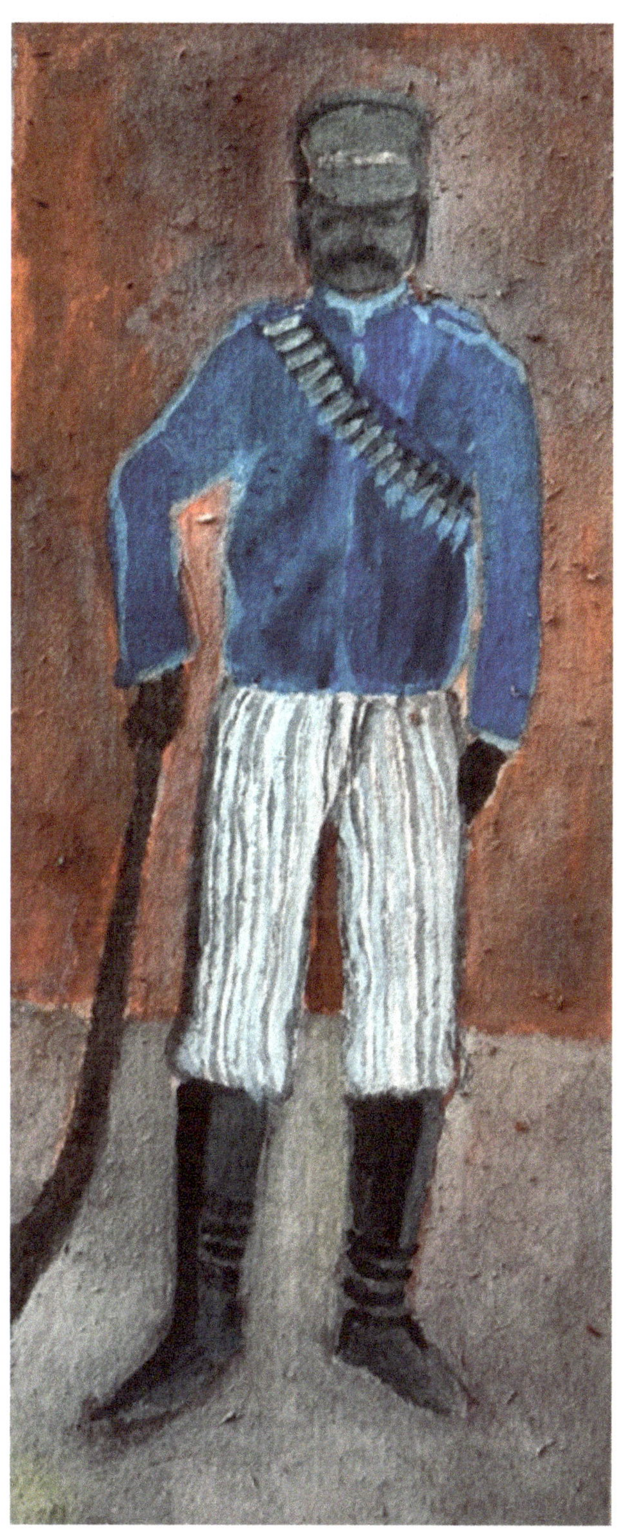

"Colonisation"

Collection: John Barclay
Medium: Oil on canvas

I made this painting (152 x 122cm) when I was at art school.
At the time I was grappling a lot with images of the land and
images associated with colonisation. Images of the British flag
and the Christian cross found their way into my paintings.

I would try to juxtapose these images with images of the land.
The outcome was this strange painting with a suggestion of a
pukamani pole side by side with the almost scarecrow-like
Christian cross.

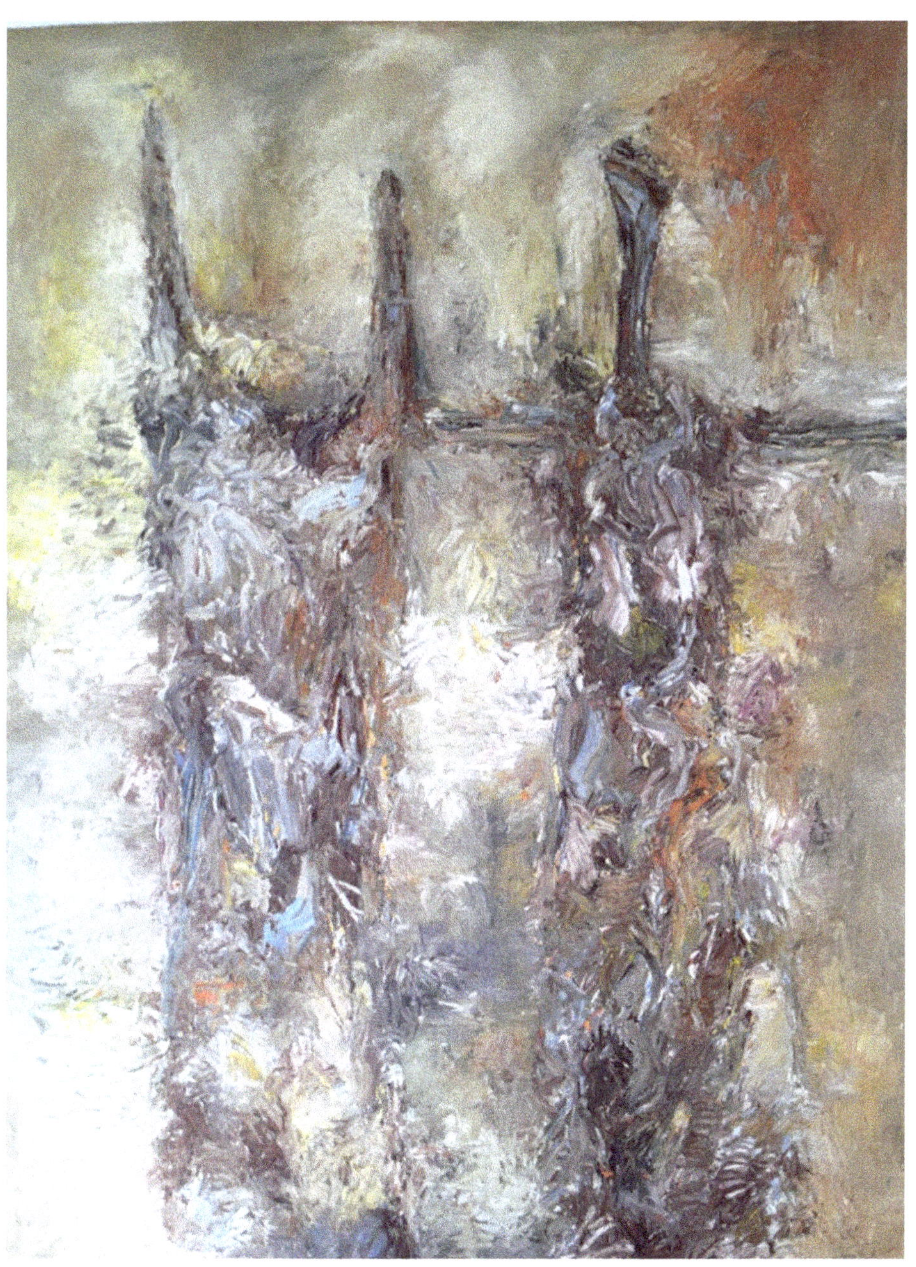

Chapter 6

Miscellaneous

"Ned Kelly Armour"

Medium: Gouache sketch on paper

Bushrangers in the time of the Australian gold rushes were a new generation of outlaws. Some of them were Frank Gardiner, Ben Hall, Captain Moonlite and Ned Kelly.

They were usually thieves by choice, after all, gold was a huge attraction. While every effort was made to protect the gold, there was the strong possibility that a Gold Escort could be "held up" and robbed by bushrangers.

While bushrangers might have been villains some became heroes in Australia's legendary past.

My sketch of Ned Kelly's armour was an illustration for my book *Blood Gold: Native Police, Bushrangers, and Law and Order on the Goldfields.*

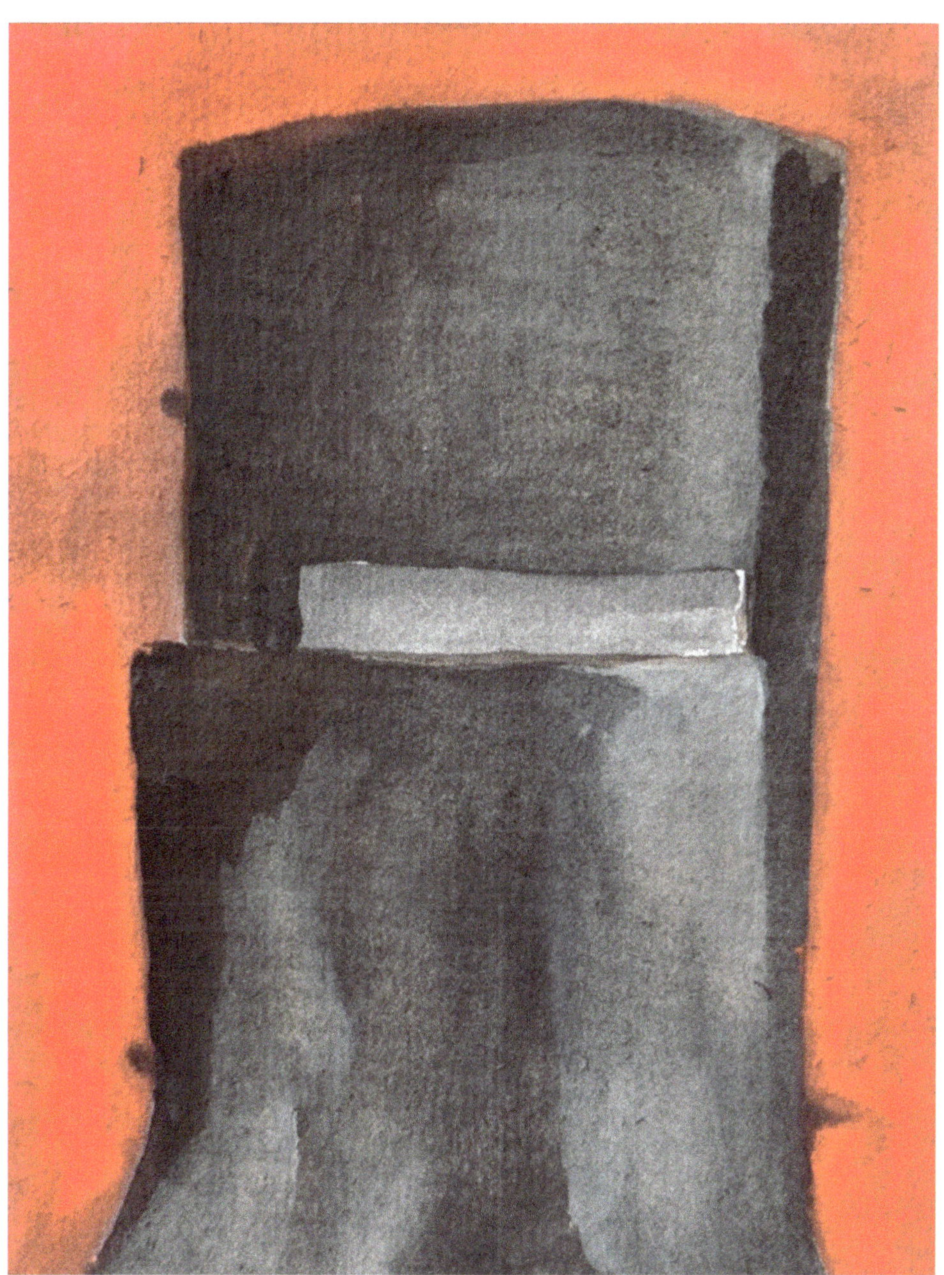

"Roman Catacombs"

Medium: Oil on canvas

In 1989 Alex and I travelled overseas to Spain, France and Italy.

When in Rome we visited the subterranean world of the catacombs which gives a glimpse into the spiritual life and art of burial of the early Christians.

The catacombs of Rome are an enigmatic portal to this ancient past and I was inspired to create this little oil painting.

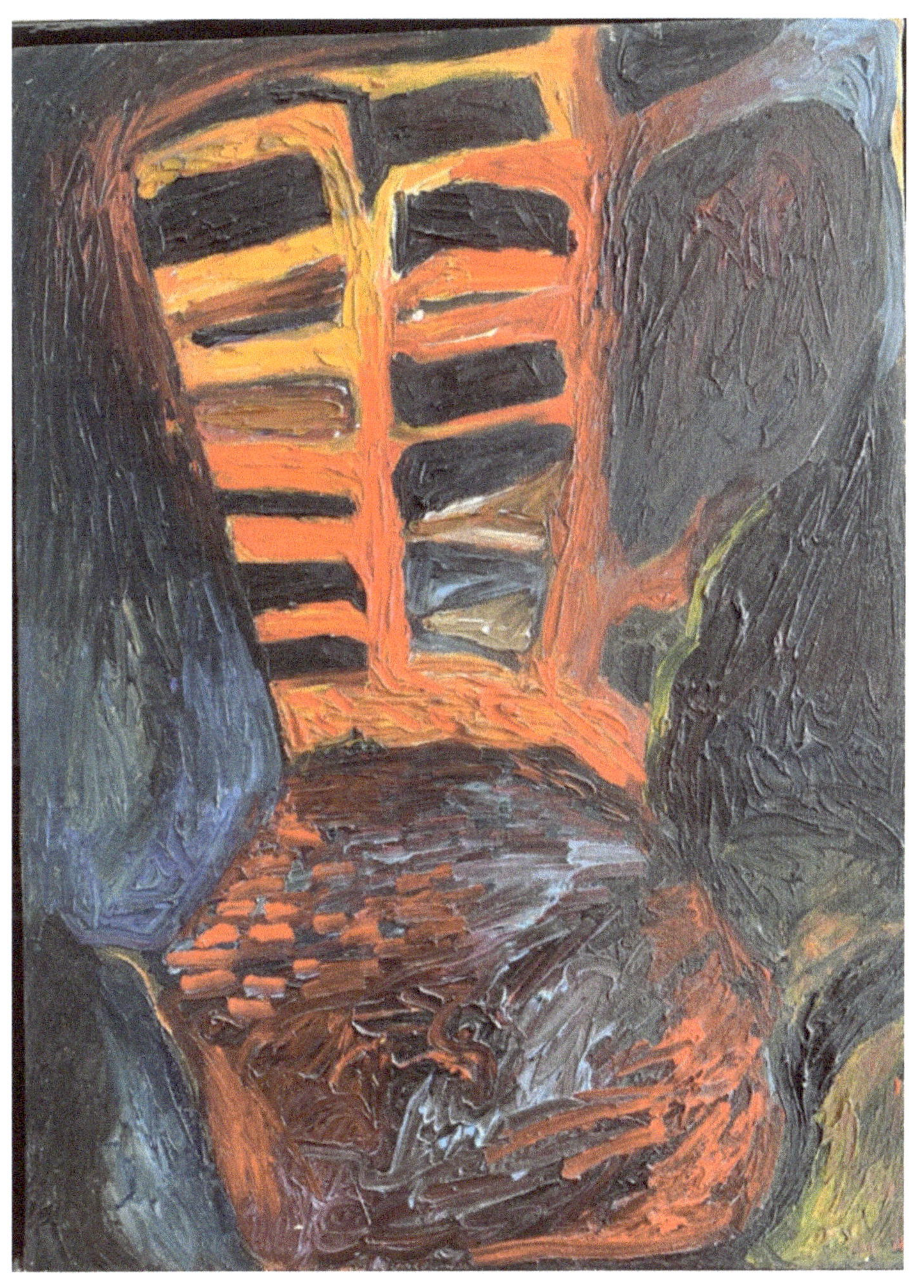

"Fashion Parade"

Medium: Oil painting

My art career started early in life when as a toddler I found the shoe polish and painted a mural on my parent's freshly covered wallpaper in the new family home at Southport on the river.

Some years later when I was about seven, I won first prize for a drawing I exhibited at the Southport agricultural show.

Then in my teens and for two years in a row, I won the Sunday Mail Child Art Competition in Queensland for my age category. My two winning paintings got full coverage in colour in the Sunday newspaper.

One of these paintings "Fashion Parade" was based on an event that I attended at the Surfers Paradise Hotel on the corner of Cavill Avenue and Surfers Paradise Boulevard in the early 1960s. This was the first oil painting I'd ever made. I was 15 years old.

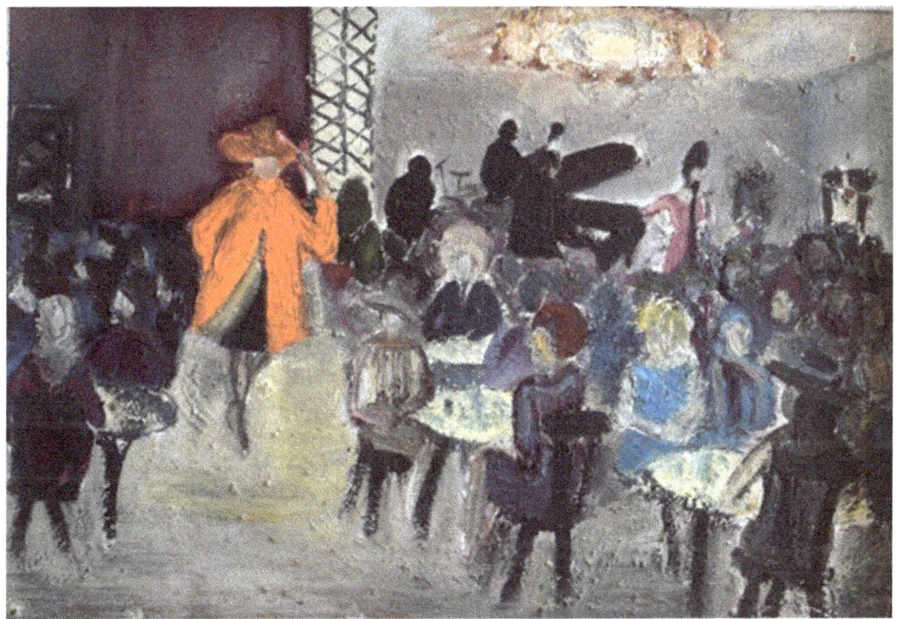

"Life Outback"

Medium: Oil on masonite

When I was 16, I won the Sunday Mail Art competition for the second time. Again, my winning painting got printed in colour in the Sunday Mail.

The painting depicts outback life at the *Kelvington* sheep station owned by Mr & Mrs Tomlinson. This was near Mungindi in Queensland, not far from Moree in New South Wales.

As a young kid I often stayed there and was cared for by their daughter, Pattie Houston.

To get to the toilet you had to walk from the homestead gate across the yard to the outdoor loo. I was very young, and it was always an adventure getting there as I had to navigate my way around the rooster that used to chase me.

This was the first of my paintings to have an Indigenous Australian theme. Unfortunately, the only image of this painting that survives is this photograph of a newspaper clipping that I found in an old scrap book.

I painted this on treated masonite and used plastic paint and tree roots to create a rugged texture.

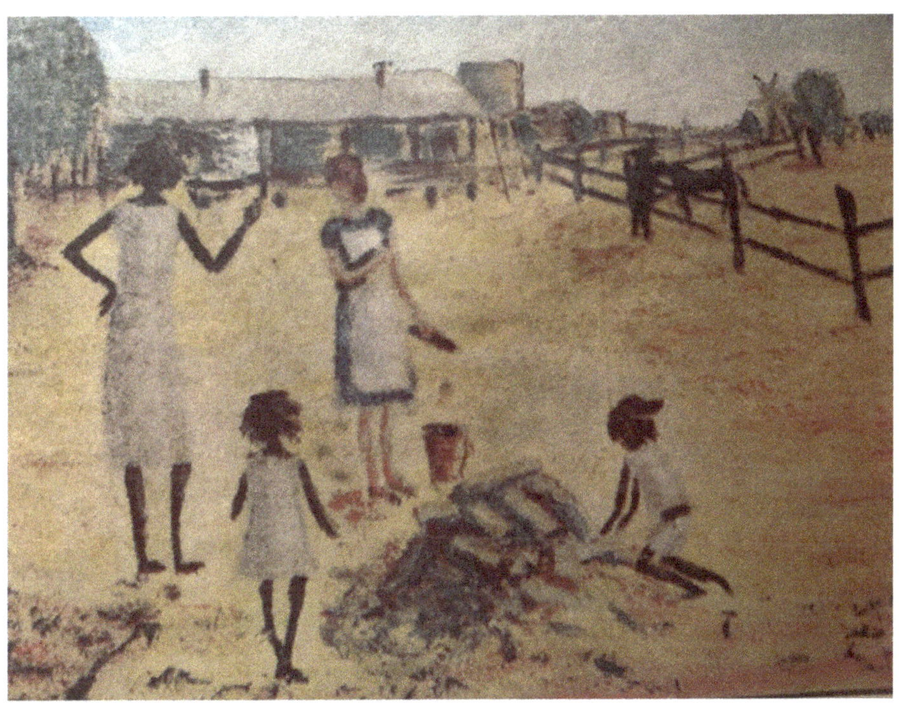

"Lifeguard Tower, Surfers Paradise"

Collection: Surfers Paradise Catholic Parish
Medium: Acrylic on canvas

A feature of Gold Coast beaches is the iconic Lifeguard Tower. Over forty towers are dotted along 52 kilometres of beaches from Coolangatta to the northern tip of the Gold Coast.

For over 85 years there has been a lifeguard service on the Gold Coast and then, in 1989, the yellow-topped towers were spaced along beaches patrolling them from Rainbow Bay to The Spit Seaway.

I spent a lot of my early life on the Surfers Paradise beach. I remember my earliest prize-winning coloured drawing was the patrolled beach and a lifesaver rescuing a young swimmer caught in a rip.

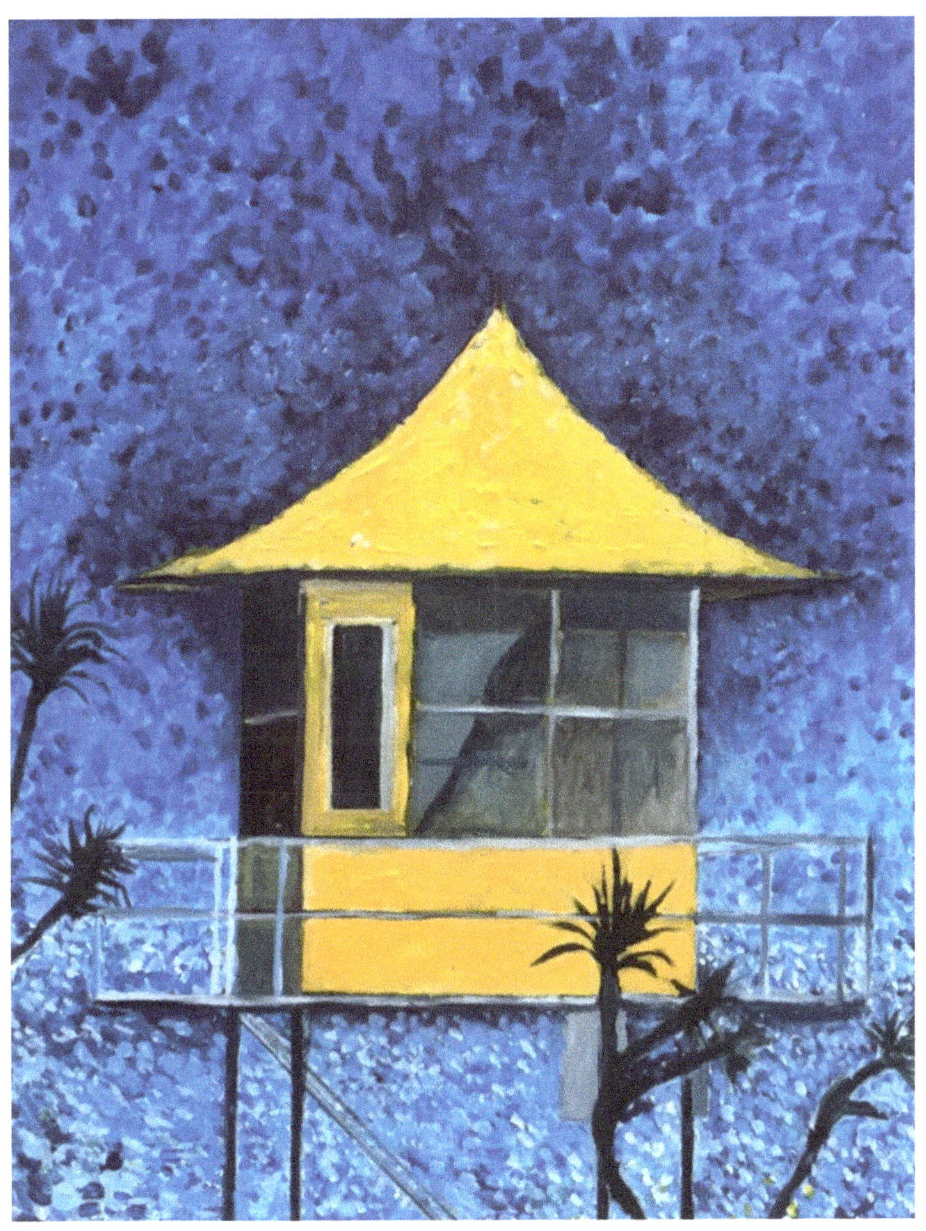

"Sydney Opera House"

Art card
Medium: Gouache on paper

In 2007 when Alex Barlow and I were living in Mosman Bay in Sydney I got the idea to create greeting cards. I started creating small images – art cards – of the local Mosman area and the Northern Beaches.

I found a market for these in various outlets in and around Mosman.

One of these greeting cards featured the Sydney Opera House. There is a magnificent view of it looking across the harbour from Cremorne Point.

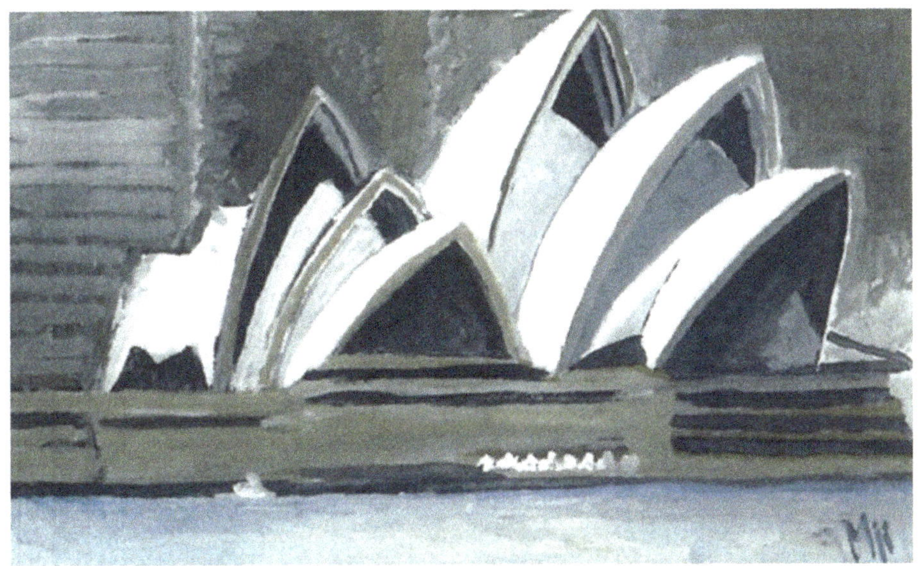

"Lighthouse at Cremorne Point"

Collection: Hill Family
Medium: Acrylic on hardboard

For many years prior to living at Mosman Bay, I would visit my family in Mosman. My brother had a huge Federation mansion that overlooked the bay.

I loved to explore the terraced gardens that went down from the house to the walking trails that wound around the water's edge. I regularly went walking along the track to Cremorne Point to view the iconic lighthouse.

I made this painting of the lighthouse in 1979 which was a few years prior to going to art school. In this era most of my paintings were realistic.

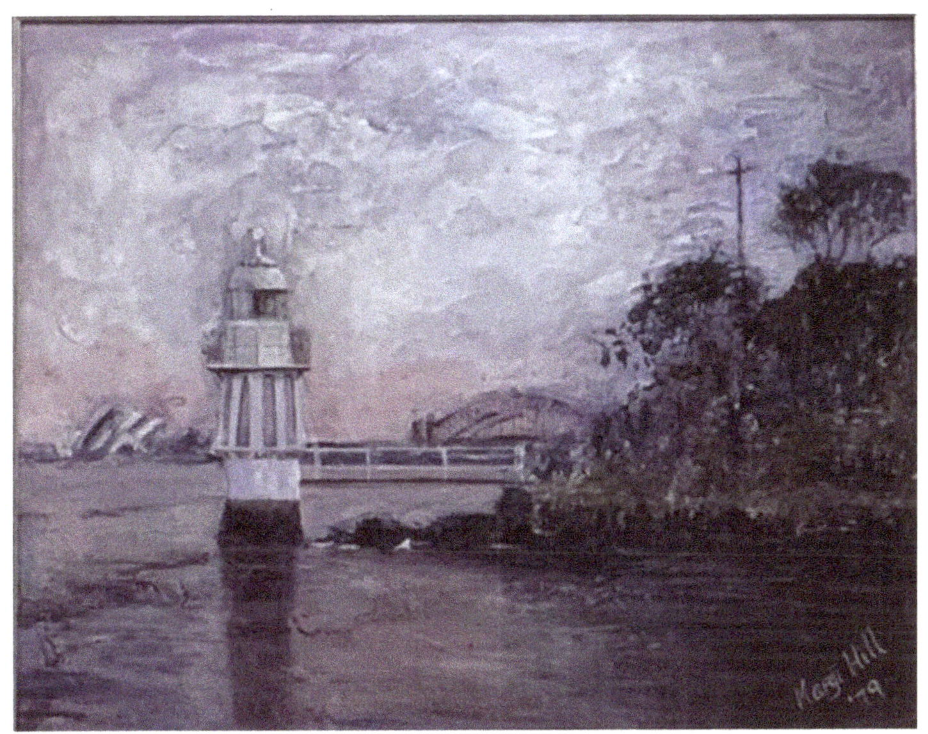

Chapter 7

Fun

"Unicorn"

Medium: Gouache sketch on paper

Sometimes it's fun just to relax and paint light-hearted themes. As you can see a lot of my artwork deals with confronting themes from Australia's hidden history.

It's nice at times just to play, so I came up with some fanciful subject matter like this unicorn.

Painting can be fun. You don't have to create wonderful works of art to have a good time. You can have fun experimenting with paint, relax with it, and let the creative juices have free expression.

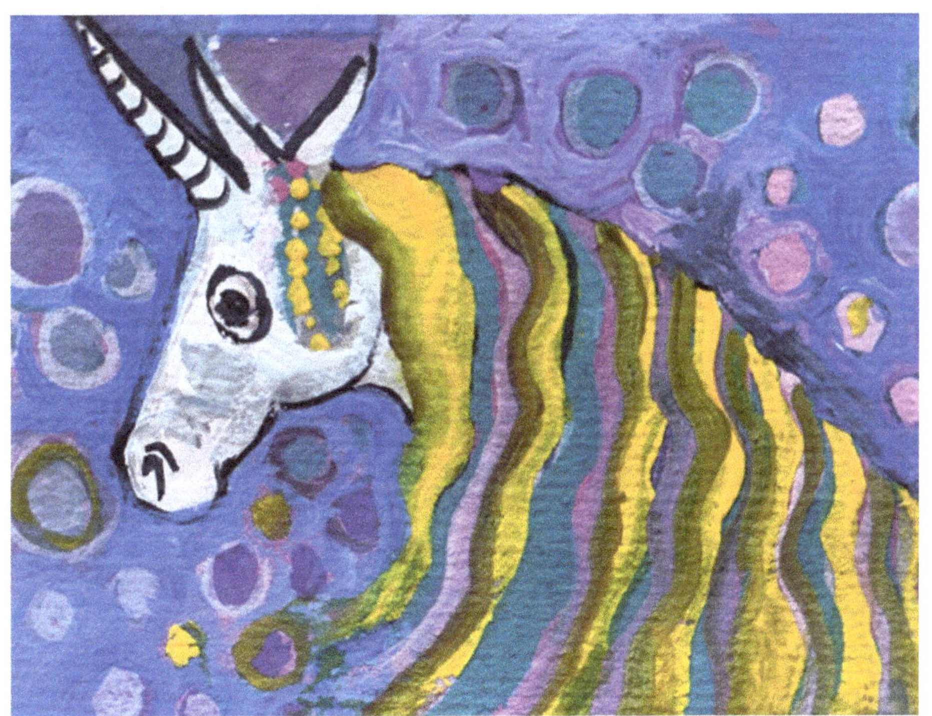

"Winston the Koala"

Medium: Gouache sketch on paper

I thought about creating a picture book for children. I came up with the idea of a koala character.

While I played around with this, the children's picture book still hasn't come to fruition.

I got as far as creating the character and this was Winston the Koala.

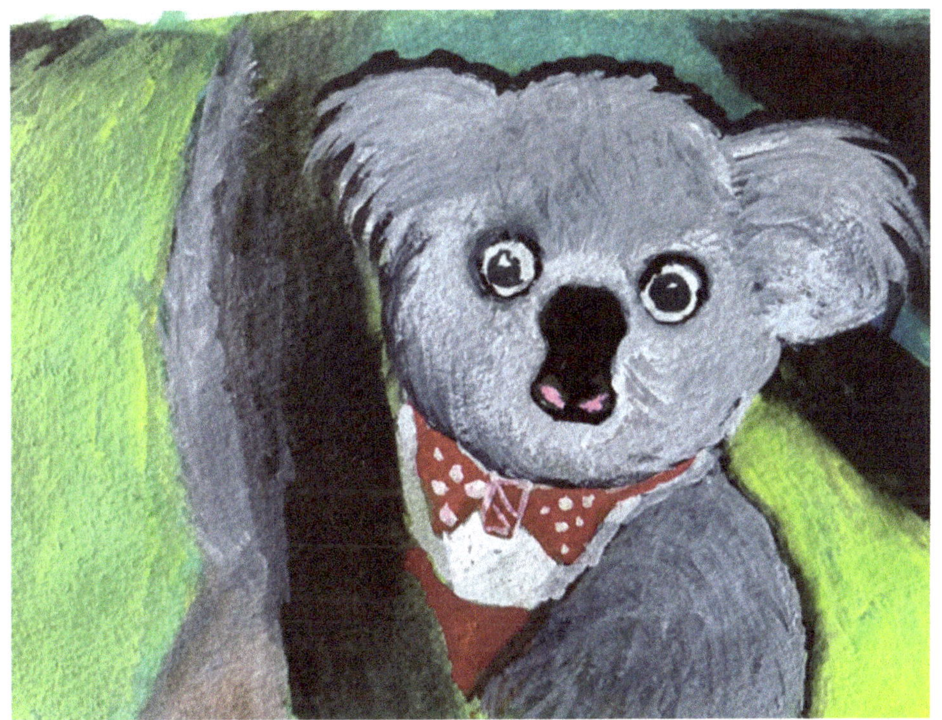

"Goanna and Winston the Koala"

Medium: Gouache sketch on paper

I wanted Winston the Koala to have friends, so I came up with other Australian characters.

His first friend was the goanna, so I painted a goanna up a tree with Winston looking on.

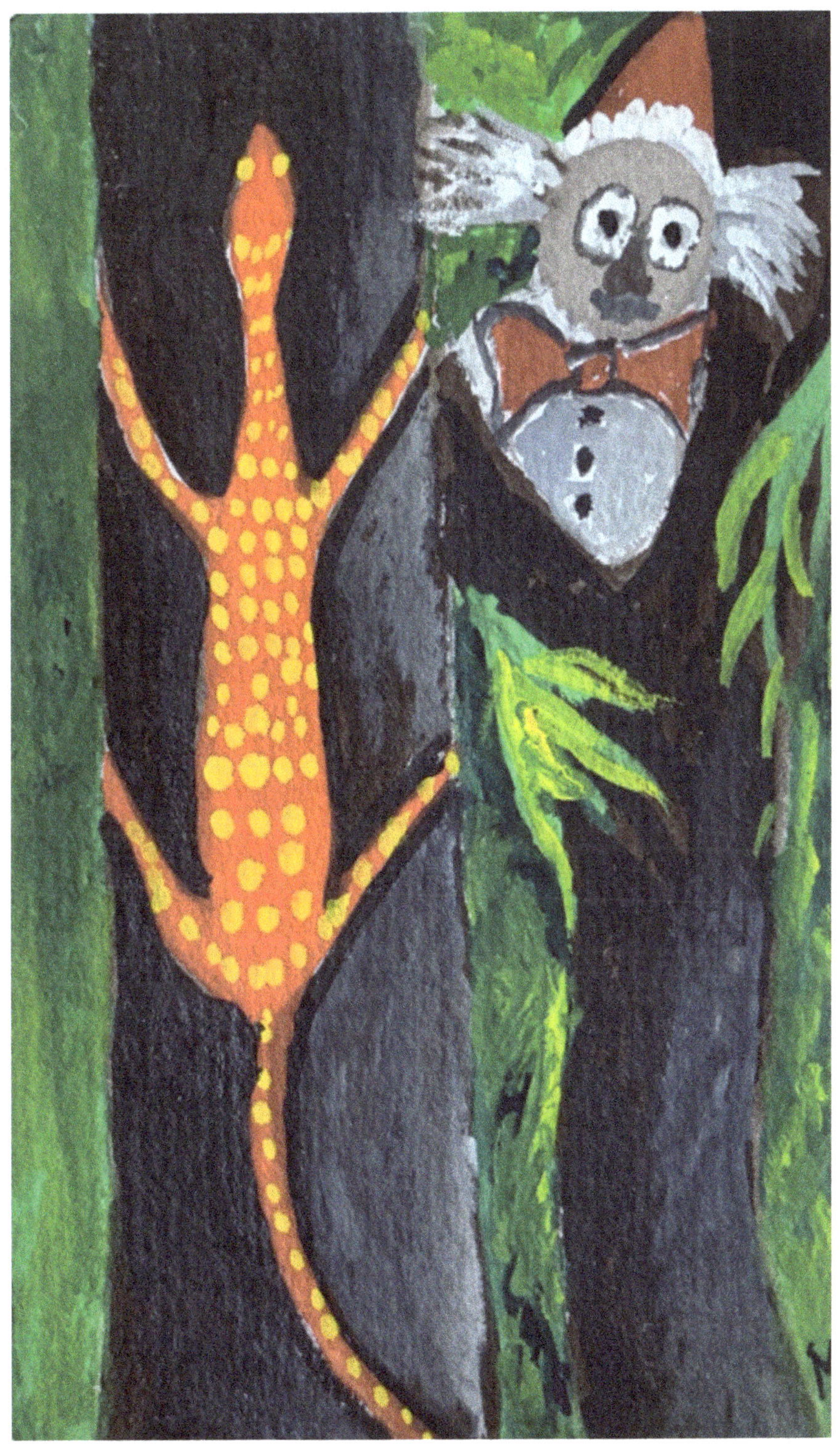

"Dolphin"

Medium: Gouache sketch on paper

Then I added another friend - this time a character from the ocean.

The dolphin was born.

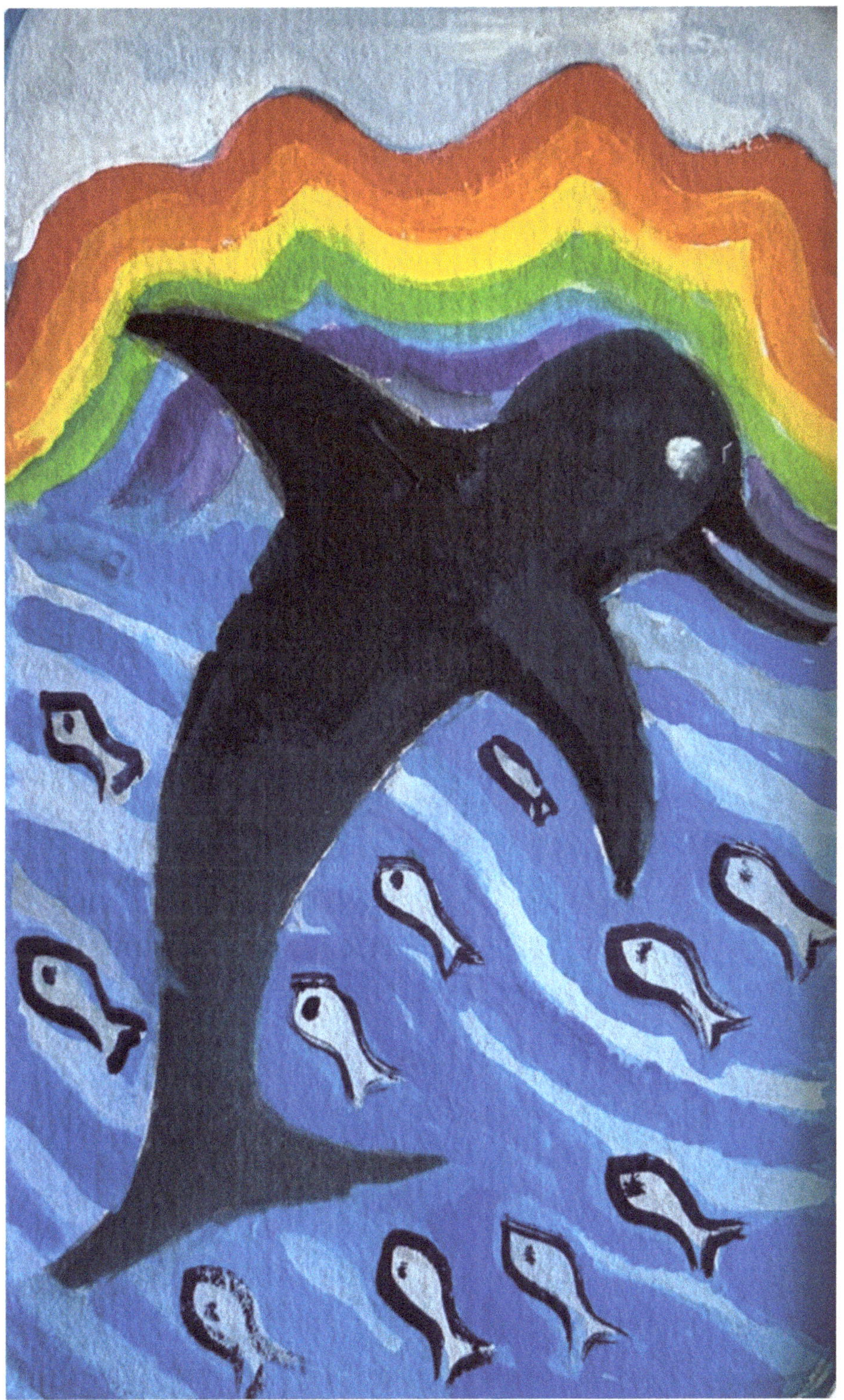

Chapter 8

Flowers

"Bird of Paradise"

Art card
Medium: Gouache on paper

In addition to painting images of the Northern Beaches and the Mosman area, I started my flower series.

You may wonder at my painting flowers when so much of my artwork has had to do with Australian history and serious issues confronting Australian society.

I got into painting flowers because much of my early life was spent in my mother's florist shop. In 1947 my mother, Doreen Hill, founded *Lotus Bud* – the flower shop. She eventually had five florist shops in Southport, Sundale, Surfers Paradise, Burleigh Heads, and Coolangatta.

As a small girl I spent a lot of time in the flower shop in Nerang Street, Southport. Most afternoons after school I would walk from St Hilda's Girls School along Nerang Street to *Lotus Bud*.

Often, I spent time in Mum's Surfers Paradise shop. This was located in the central shopping area. While the beach was always the main attraction for visitors coming to Surfers Paradise, there was a vibrant shopping area with its network of narrow arcades linking the main drag to Orchid Avenue. In one of these arcades my mother's flower shop was combined with an impressive garden centre at the end of the arcade going into Orchid Avenue.

As a result of spending a lot of time with flowers, I certainly developed a great love of them.

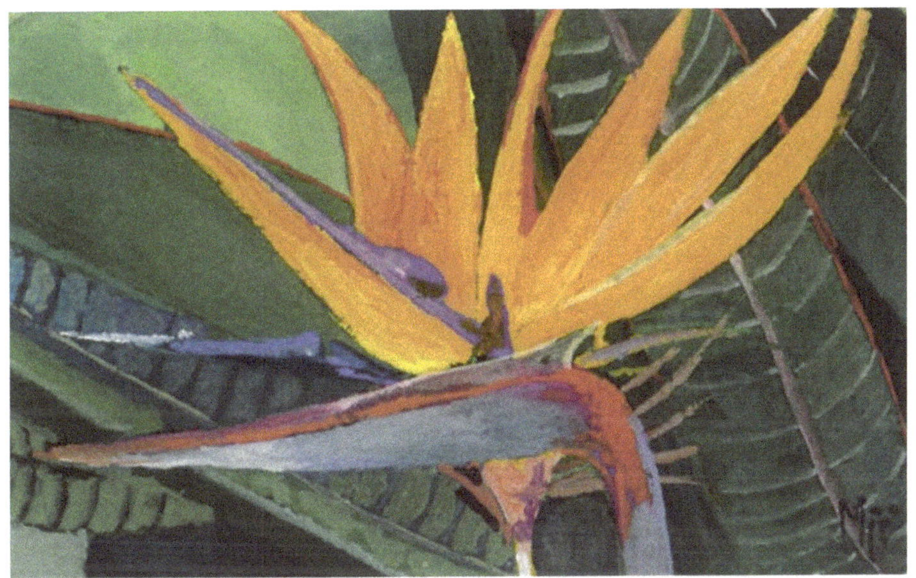

"Hibiscus"

Art card
Medium: Gouache on paper

The hibiscus flower dominated the Gold Coast flora when I was growing up. It was also part of the flora at Mosman Bay.

When Alex and I lived at Mosman Bay I regularly walked around the foreshores of the bay to Cremorne Point.

The trail started at the end of Avenue Road in Mosman, meandered around past the Mosman Rowers, and along through all the verdant, sub-tropical undergrowth. You would take in the harbour views, and old Federation houses, pass through historic gardens, and then along to the Robertsons Point Lighthouse.

Along the walking trail, there were always beautiful flowers in bloom, and that is where I came across the flowering hibiscus.

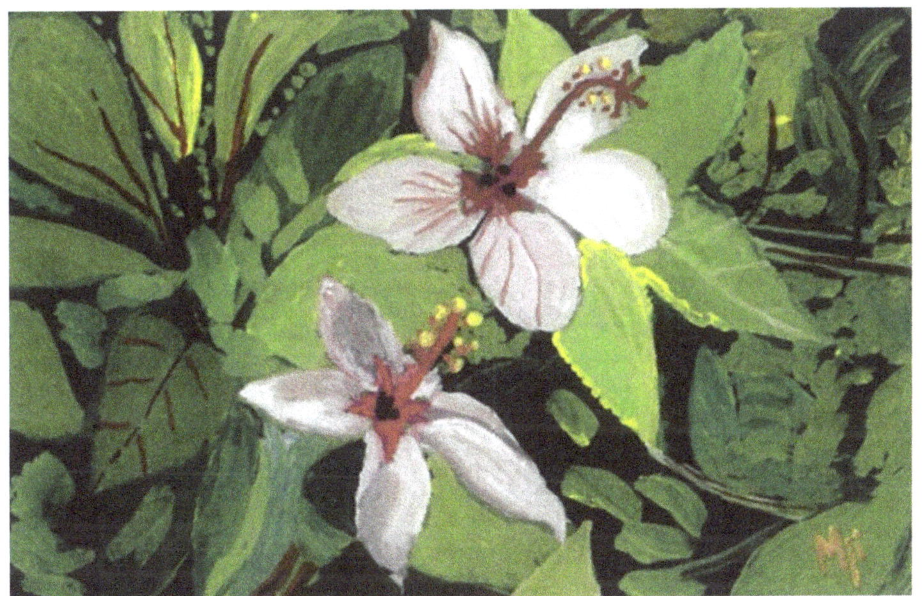

"Cymbidium Orchid"

Art card
Medium: Gouache on paper

When I meandered along the walking trail through the Cremorne Point Reserve I would come across the Lex and Ruby Graham Gardens. These were nothing short of magical.

In this part of the world, you feel as if the Sydney CBD is a faraway place.

You've stepped back in time into a setting that is jungle-like with its huge, lush and towering foliage. Around here I came across the regal and elegant cymbidium orchid.

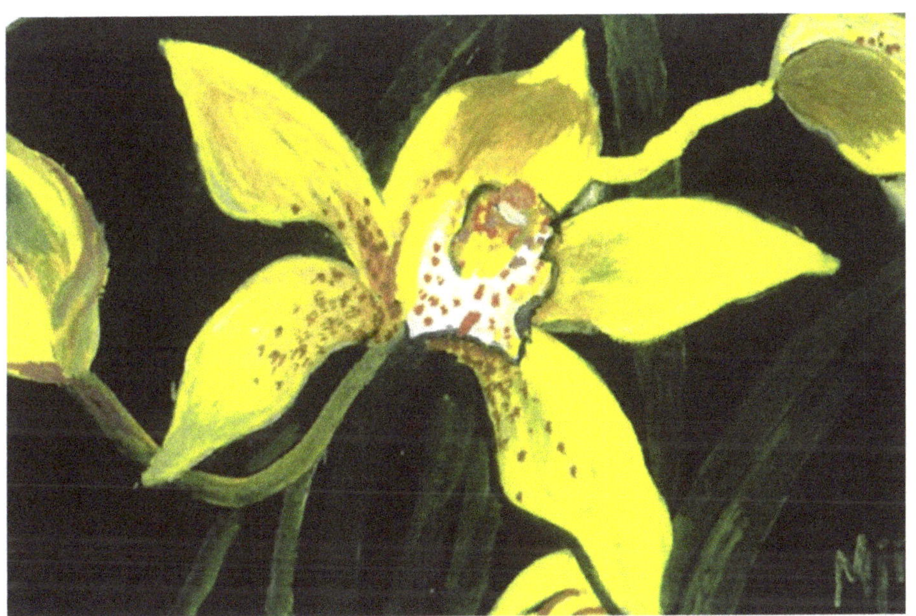

"Bottle Brush"

Art card
Medium: Gouache on paper

Along the walking trail is the yellow bottle brush, *Melaleuca pallida* which is part of the myrtle family endemic to eastern Australia. You find it on the harbour-side paths which wind through gardens and sections of native bushland.

I used to love to sit on a bench seat nearby and take in the spectacular water views.

This walking trail is the perfect place to view the massive ocean liners as they glide up Sydney Harbour and then dock at the Overseas Passenger Terminal at Circular Quay.

Anyone passionate about ship watching can see the daily traffic of ships and sea vessels arriving and departing the harbour.

It's incredible to watch a container-loaded cargo vessel or multi-deck cruise ship navigate gently up the harbour and slide elegantly past the harbour beaches and suburbs like Mosman Bay and Cremorne Point.

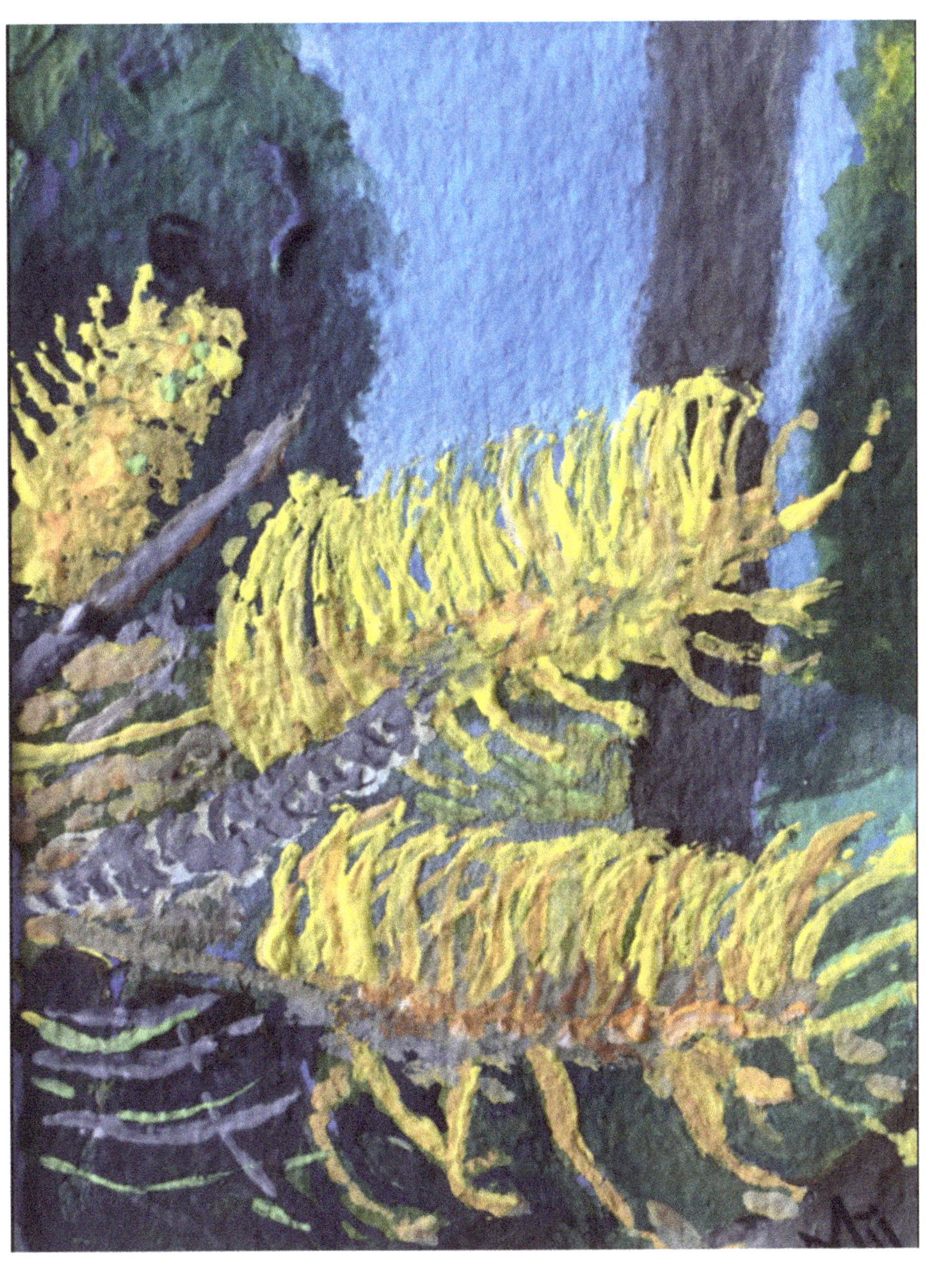

About Marji Hill

Artist & Author

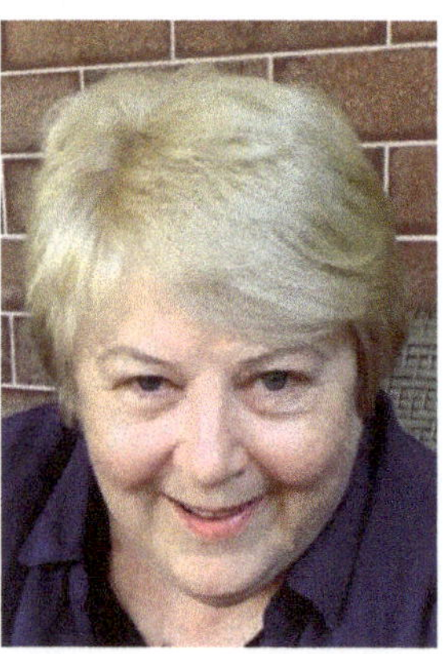

Marji Hill, an artist and painter since childhood, runs her art career alongside her career as an author.

She is a highly respected international author as well as a seasoned business executive, researcher and coach.

Marji is passionate about promoting understanding between Australia's first people and other Australians.

The spirit of reconciliation was fostered in all her writings ever since she was a Research Fellow in Education at the Australian Institute of Aboriginal and Torres Strait Islander Studies (AIATSIS) in Canberra.

From 2008 to 2011, Marji was Deputy Chairperson of the Mosman Branch of Reconciliation Australia in Sydney.

Following her Research Fellowship at AIATSIS in 1976 Marji, together with her late partner, Alex Barlow, produced more than seventy (70) books on all aspects of the First Nations people including the critical, annotated bibliography *Black Australia*.

In 1989 she was the Project Coordinator and one of the researchers and writers of *Australian Aboriginal Culture* the official Australian Government publication on First Nations people.

In 1988 *Six Australian Battlefields* was published by Angus and Robertson. A decade later it was re-published by Allen & Unwin as a paperback edition.

Her nine-volume encyclopaedia, *Macmillan Encyclopaedia of Australia's Aboriginal Peoples* was published in 2000 and in 2009 she published *The Apology: Saying Sorry To The Stolen Generations.*

Marji's more recent publications extend to self-improvement and self-help with books like *Staying Young Growing Old* and *Inspired by Country* a self-help book about painting with gouache.

Marji's artworks range from very large oil paintings on canvas to very small works on paper — gouache being a favourite medium.

Black/white relations, reconciliation, Eureka, and the discovery of gold are common themes not only in her writings but also in her art.

Her small paintings are simple responses to land and sea environments.

Painting has been a lifetime passion for Marji. Her formal art training took place in the 1980s at the Canberra School of Art which in 1992 became ANU School of Art & Design.

As soon as she completed her Master of Arts Degree in Anthropology at the Australian National University (ANU), Marji went on to get a Post Graduate Diploma in Painting. Since then, she held eight solo exhibitions in Canberra, Melbourne and Sydney and participated in various group shows.

One of her large paintings was included in the 2004-2005 Art Gallery of Ballarat Traveling Exhibition *Eureka Revisited: The Contest of Memories*. This exhibition travelled to Melbourne,

Canberra and Ballarat — part of the 150-year celebration of the Eureka Stockade.

Two of her large paintings were commissioned by the Citigold Corporation. One for many years hung in the foyer of Jupiter's Casino in Townsville until the casino was sold, becoming The Ville Resort-Casino.

Jupiter's Lucky Strike celebrates the discovery of gold by First Nations boy, Jupiter Mosman in 1871 at Charters Towers in North Queensland. This painting today is in the offices of the Citigold Corporation in Charters Towers.

The other, a portrait of Jupiter Mosman resides in the World Theatre in Charters Towers.

Marji's paintings are in many private collections both in Australia and overseas and she is represented in the Art Gallery of Ballarat and the Ballarat and Sydney campuses of the Australian Catholic University.

For many years Marji travelled extensively both within Australia and internationally, working as a consultant, doing speaking engagements, motivating people, and developing her art career.

Marji has returned to her birthplace and now resides in Surfers Paradise. She pursues her interests of writing, painting, coaching, publishing, and internet marketing.

More Books by Marji Hill

Self-improvement/Self-Help

Hill, Marji 2014 *Staying Young Growing Old.* Broadbeach, Qld, The Prison Tree Press.

Hill, Marji 2020 *How Big Is Your Why? An Author's Guide to Time Management and Productivity to Achieve Transformational Results.* Broadbeach, Qld, The Prison Tree Press.

Hill, Marji 2020 *A Create and Publish Toolbox: 101 Prompts In A Guided Journal To Help You Write, Self-publish, And Market Your Book On Amazon.* Broadbeach, Qld, The Prison Tree Press.

Hill, Marji 2021 *Inspired by Country: An Artist's Journey Back to Nature, Landscape Painting with Gouache.* Broadbeach, Qld, The Prison Tree Press.

First Nations

Hill, Marji 2021 *First People Then and Now: Introducing Indigenous Australians.* 2nd ed. Broadbeach, Qld, The Prison Tree Press.

Hill, Marji 2021 *Australian Aboriginal History: 5 Stories of Indigenous Heroes.* Broadbeach, Qld, The Prison Tree Press.

Gold

Hill, Marji (2022) *Gates of Gold: The Discovery of Gold, its Legacy and its Contribution to Australian Identity* Broadbeach, Qld, The Prison Tree Press.

Hill, Marji (2022) *Shadows of Gold: Eureka and the Birth of Australian Democracy.* Broadbeach, Qld, The Prison Tree Press.

Hill, Marji (2022) *Gold and the Chinese: Racism, Riots and Protest on the Australian Goldfields.* Broadbeach, Qld, The Prison Tree Press.

Hill, Marji (2022) *Ghosts of Gold: The Life and Times of Jupiter Mosman.* Broadbeach, Qld, The Prison Tree Press.

Hill, Marji (2022) *Blood Gold: Native Police, Bushrangers & Law and Order on the Goldfields.* Broadbeach, Qld, The Prison Tree Press.